HOLY MYSTERIES

ENCOUNTERING THE RISEN JESUS

The scripture quotations in this book of devotions are from The New Revised Standard Version Bible, copyright ©1989 by the Division of Christian Education of the National Council of the Churches of Christ in the U.S.A., and are used by permission. All rights reserved.

©2025 Episcopal Diocese of Georgia
All rights reserved

Cover Art

The cover painting is "Christ in the Wilderness" by Kelly Latimore and is used by permission of the artist with all rights reserved. Kelly writes of his work, "I do not wish to approach Iconography as an art form that simply follows an inherited tradition, knowledge, and practice. I want it to be a 'holy pondering', meditation, and process that potentially brings about a new way of seeing for the viewer and me." Discover his powerful artwork for yourself at kellylatimoreicons.com.

Unless otherwise noted in the caption, all other artwork in this book is courtesy of The Met, from the 492,000 of works of art that the museum has placed in the public domain. Photos are courtesy of the authors.

Holy Mysteries

Encountering the risen Jesus

Frank & Victoria Logue

Dedication

We dedicate this book to Joni Woolf, friend, and a parishioner of Calvary Episcopal Church in Americus. We are grateful for her editing this Eastertide book as well as our previous devotional *Feast of Feasts: Advent, Christmas, and Epiphany with St. Francis*. We appreciate not only Joni's editorial expertise, but also her support and encouragement.

> You call for faith:
> I show you doubt,
> to prove that faith exists.
> The more of doubt,
> the stronger faith, I say,
> if faith o'ercomes doubt.

-from *Bishop Blougram's Apology* by Robert Browning

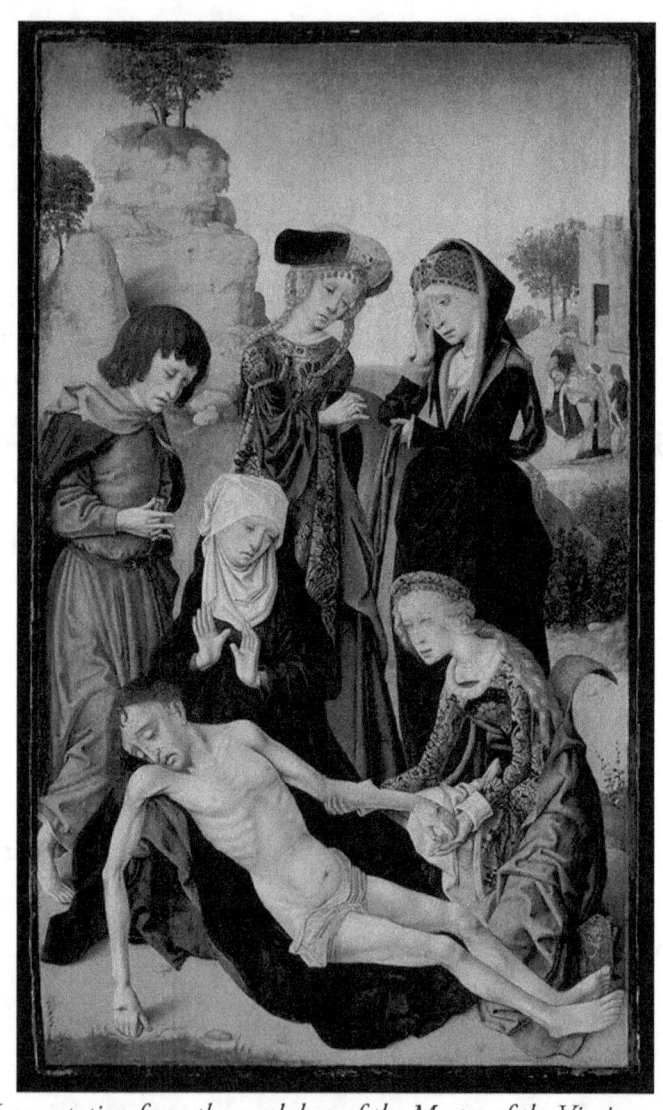

The Lamentation from the workshop of the Master of the Virgin among Virgins. (Netherlandish, active ca. 1460–95)

Introduction

"I have long been wishing,
O true-born and dearly beloved children of the Church,
to discourse to you concerning
these spiritual and heavenly Mysteries;
but since I well knew that seeing
is far more persuasive than hearing,
I waited for the present season."

-Cyril of Jerusalem's Lecture 19: *On the Mysteries I*

"To us that speak daily of the death of Christ
(he was crucified, dead, and buried),
can the memory or the mention of our own death
be irksome or bitter?"

-John Donne, in his sermon *Death's Duel*

Our story begins in the silence of the night, in a garden near the Place of the Skull. Jesus lies dead in a tomb provided by Joseph of Arimathea, a religious leader who had kept his faith in Jesus a secret until the unthinkable occurred. After Jesus had been tortured and killed, Joseph asks boldly if Pontius Pilate will let him remove his Rabbi from the cross. Jesus, who was the most gracious of hosts, was always in need of hospitality. He had described himself as the Son of Man who had nowhere to lay his head. On this longest of sabbaths for his followers, he lies wrapped in linen cloth in a new tomb where no one had ever been laid.

The disciples who scattered on Jesus' arrest are joined by John and Jesus' Mother, Mary, and the other women who stayed near their hoped-for Messiah when he suffered and died. They are back in the upper room where they had all celebrated the Passover on an evening that must have felt a lifetime ago. Everything had changed so quickly in the day that followed.

This is not a "once upon a time story." That there was a historic person named Jesus of Nazareth is as well-documented as the lives of other historic people of his time. Besides the Bible, we have records of Jesus from other sources, especially from people who were not Christians. Both the Roman historians Tacitus and Suetonius wrote about Jesus, as did the Jewish historian Josephus. Jesus was an itinerant preacher known for working miracles who was proclaimed as a Messiah before being put to death as a threat to the status quo in the uneasy peace of Jerusalem.

Jesus was not the first or last person hailed as the promised anointed one, the Messiah. The unusual part of the story is that he is remembered by more than a few experts on the history of the Ancient Near East. The Jesus Movement persisting centuries after his death is what points us back to that Upper Room in Jerusalem on that first Sunday morning and again the next week when Thomas was present.

Encountering the risen Jesus

Something happened that transformed human history as the first followers of Jesus experienced something so amazing that they gave the rest of their lives to spreading the Good News. They tell us that Jesus appeared among them and said, "Peace be with you."

That the disciples did not go home and continue the lives they had before encountering Jesus is the first proof we have for resurrection. Something transformed their lives and sustained them for the persecution that followed. Jesus' first followers did not have to tell a story of resurrection at all for their movement to continue. Neither Buddha's followers nor those of Muhammad made such a claim of appearing bodily resurrected. The disciples proclaimed Jesus' resurrection, not because everyone expected this of the Messiah, but because it was so life-changingly unexpected that they couldn't avoid talking about it. It would have been easier if they had just claimed that Jesus' message was still valid; that his teaching should live on. But that is not what they said. The apostles preached that Jesus was and is the firstborn of the dead; the until now still unrepeatable example of the resurrection to come at the end of time.

We wrote this book of devotions to allow us to spend the Great Fifty Days from Easter to Pentecost reflecting on the resurrection through the lenses of scripture and the early church tradition of teaching about the holy mysteries of the sacraments in Easter Week. We weave together the strands of the resurrection appearances found in the Bible with the teachings of some of the notable witnesses to this Easter season throughout church history. Each week, you will read two of the fourteen scriptural texts that make up the Stations of the Resurrection.

We also bring in early Christian teaching. Cyril of Jerusalem gave his five mystagogical lectures to the newly baptized in The Church of the Holy Sepulchre. These well-documented lectures on holy mysteries by the Bishop of Jerusalem bring us into the Church of the Resurrection to learn of the sacraments of baptism, Eucharist, and confirmation as they were taught in the Fourth Century. Given this was a few decades after the Emperor Constantine ended the persecution of Christians with his Edict of Milan in 313, these texts preserve the understanding of the sacraments at this important moment in church history.

A personal reflection each week on how we have encountered Jesus is also shared with you in the hope of prompting you to consider the ways, both mundane and surprising, when you have experienced the risen Jesus. As we move through these meditations from sacred mysteries through the sacraments to vocation, we also want to encourage you to encounter Jesus in new ways.

Week 1
Mystery

Monday – Introducing Mystery

We (the authors) enjoy mystery novels with the quirky, yet determined, detective doggedly pursuing clues to discover the truth. Agatha Christie's Miss Marple is a fun twist on the gentleman detective. She is a careful observer of human behavior who knows the people of her village of St. Mary Mead so well that it gives insight into all people. She sees through the lies people tell to the character of the person beneath the surface as revealed in little inconsistencies. Across sixty-six novels and fourteen short-story collections, Christie offered every permutation on the twist ending for a murder mystery from every suspect as one of the killers to every suspect dying.

Movies, television, and novels are full of mystery. Just as the sun once never set on the British flag, the TV show Law and Order and its spin-offs are always playing in reruns on some channel 24/7/365. Within the hour, the truth is revealed and justice served. While acknowledging issues that can arise in the justice system, the viewer is consistently soothed that most everything is well as we are in the hands of the good guys who usually end up getting it right. For the two of us, this is not our favorite form of whodunit.

We love to read a sub-genre of novels usually called Nordic Noir. These morally complex books, set in the bleak landscapes of Scandinavia are not such a sharp departure for us as Victoria always enjoyed Ed McBain's police procedurals. Many see McBain's 87th Precinct stories as a source for these straightforward narratives about the monotonous, day-to-day work of police that results in uncovering a killer. The prose is as bare as the scenery in these dark mysteries that void metaphor in favor of a Joe Friday just-the-facts style. The bland surface covers the secret hatreds to contrast the Scandinavian ideals of social justice and liberalism with the reality of misogyny, racism, and xenophobia.

Authors like Iceland's Arnaldur Indriðason and Norway's Karin Fossum are less interested in whodunit than in revealing the why that comes from the inner life of the people populating an isolated village where the unspeakable has happened. The relatively low crime rate allows for a detective to push forward at a glacial speed not just to an arrest, but to an understanding that often still eludes the detective. Nordic Noir usually avoids tidy endings.

All of these types of stories inform our understanding of mystery, but they bear only the slightest resemblance to mystery as we mean it when we say "The Holy Trinity is a sacred mystery" or when we write of the Holy Mysteries of the sacraments. Here we hope that the contrast between Miss Marple and Law and Order as they contrast with

Encountering the risen Jesus

Scandinavian crime fiction is instructive.

The goal in the examples of Agatha Christie and television procedurals is to explain the mystery. The dogged detective, or the team of police and attorneys, discover The Answer. The mystery is a riddle with a single, set solution. It was: Colonel Mustard in the library with the candlestick. The cold-hearted fiction from the north shows that there is always more to learn. Even if Miss Marple understands her village completely from her own perspective, she still does not conceive all that her butcher knows, or what the returned war veteran who can't keep consistent work sees. We learn that it is beyond the powers of detection to fully appreciate how a murder transpired in this case, and in another instance an even more despicable person maintains a careful façade to be lionized on their death by natural causes. There is more present in the lives of even a tiny, isolated village than one can comprehend, much less in our actual circles of family, friends, and co-workers. This comes closer to the Holy Mysteries.

We work throughout our lives to learn more and more about ourselves only to find that we learned something a stranger knows about us within the first five minutes. We hardly know ourselves. Likewise, those close to us have parts we don't fully see or appreciate. How much more is there to discover about the Triune God who made us and loves us and wants us to journey further into the very heart of the Divine!

The early Christian Church tradition of teaching mystagogy (initiating one into sacred mysteries) was not about a one-time revelation of something that had been hidden, but an ever-deepening understanding of something we know in part. Sitting with a teacher like Cyril of Jerusalem for five to seven classes in Easter Week was meant to open the path to a sacramental life. The sacraments have the potential to lead us to become more Christ-like over time. This is the work of a lifetime and beyond.

- Do you prefer set answers or there being ever more to discover?
- How has your understanding of God changed over time?

Tuesday – Frank's Reflection

My heart raced as I was unable to catch my breath. With a rock-solid certainty that I was dying, I dashed up the stairs and into my parents' bedroom, where they, once again, assured me that I would live to see the new day. For many years, I was a seemingly incurable hypochondriac trapped by the fear of my own mortality.

This began with a long hospital stay that scarred my psyche. When I was eight, I contracted the mumps. I returned to school the next week only to be sent home on the first day back after throwing up. I went home and napped. I woke up in the emergency room at a hospital in Atlanta as they were giving me a spinal tap. I would be in and out of a coma before I learned I had encephalitis. Doctors could treat the symptoms, but there was no cure. I lived in Crawford Long Hospital for two months, before finally returning to school, still having grand mal seizures on occasion that sometimes terrified classmates when they happened while I was at school. Those would eventually stop, but the whole experience marked me. I was much more fearful than any of my family and friends, practically paralyzed at times by my fear of death.

I would have panic attacks from time to time into my teens, twenties, and early thirties with my heart beating rapidly and breathing getting shallow and rapid as I was confronted again with the certainty of my death. I tried finding refuge in the idea of The Rapture, placing my hopes in Jesus returning before I died as a kind of get-out-of-mortality-free card.

Growing up at Mount Paran Church of God from the age of ten until I left for college at seventeen, an image of The Rapture I first encountered there captured my imagination. Quite commonly found in Christian bookstores in the late 1970s, the painting was a fixture of my early teen years. It showed Jesus hovering in the sky as people floated up to heaven to meet their Lord leaving behind car and airplane wrecks as well as empty graves. I tried to think happy thoughts of life in heaven, but year after year of worshiping sounded like it would get boring fast. I just didn't want to die.

The Rapture was also a two-edged sword as it gave me the possibility of getting into heaven without death and yet it came with the fear of being left behind. I couldn't quite hold on to the vision of the joy of being united with Jesus. The God I knew then was a big meanie, hell-bent on punishing us for even accidentally putting a toe over the line of the commandments. Many years before the books and movies of the *Left Behind* series, I was obsessed with the terrifying thoughts of life on earth after Jesus' return for those not taken into heaven.

My fear did not keep me from trying skydiving or hiking the length of the Appalachian Trail. I wasn't exactly risk-averse. The true, very deep fear was that the mortality rate for humans is one-hundred percent. The inevitability of death was what oppressed me. The bondage to that paralyzing fear lifted for me during a youth group meeting at St. Peter's Episcopal Church in Rome, Georgia. In the mid-1990s, Victoria and I led the high school youth group as parishioners of the congregation. A member of the group, 16-year-old Tannika, wanted to be baptized. As the youth group was her real community within the church, the baptism service was scheduled during our youth time with the youth group joining Tannika's mom in presenting her for baptism. Everyone gathered for the liturgy served as presenters for Tannika. Victoria and I gladly accepted her request that we serve as her Godparents.

Just as Tannika was baptized, her head still dripping baptismal waters on the floor, the Rev. Al Daviou said a prayer and then made the sign of the cross on Tannika's forehead with the oil of chrism saying, "Tannika, you are sealed by the Holy Spirit in baptism and marked as Christ's own forever."

There are moments in life when a holy mystery is made real as a veil is pulled back. You get a glimpse of something deeply true that is difficult to express in words. In this moment of being sealed by the Holy Spirit, I felt the connectedness of all time and space, all creation. That moment with those words was such a transcendent experience and I saw the truth that eternity is not in the future tense, but ever present. We talk about eternal life as if it were a distant possibility, something we hope to have in the future. Yet the promise of scripture is eternal life that starts right here, right now. In Tannika's baptism, she made a public faith commitment with eternal consequences. Though I pray that Tannika outlives me, I know I will die and so will she. Yet the death that awaits her holds no power over Tannika, for she was unbound that day at St. Peter's and so was I.

In the years since that transcendent baptism, I have been the one to say those words over more than 150 new Christians. I have also been at the bedside of many people as they faced death with a deep faith that inspires me. Barring an accident, massive heart attack, or some other way of being surprised by death, we are understudies for the role of the one whose health is failing and for whom death is an imminent threat. You and I will come to our own Gethsemane as we face our mortality through suffering. I don't look forward to decline and death. But the knowledge that eternal life has already started set me free from those panic attacks. The time we experience exists within eternity. All of space and time is held in the heart of the Holy Trinity. This is a mystery whose depths I can not plumb, but it is grounded in the reality that the one in whom we live and move and have our being inhabits eternity.

- How do you conceive of eternity?
- Have you seen someone face their death in ways that inspire you?

Wednesday – The Earthquake

"After the sabbath, as the first day of the week was dawning, Mary Magdalene and the other Mary went to see the tomb. And suddenly there was a great earthquake; for an angel of the Lord, descending from heaven, came and rolled back the stone and sat on it. His appearance was like lightning, and his clothing white as snow. For fear of him the guards shook and became like dead men. But the angel said to the women, 'Do not be afraid; I know that you are looking for Jesus who was crucified. He is not here; for he has been raised, as he said. Come, see the place where he lay. Then go quickly and tell his disciples, 'He has been raised from the dead, and indeed he is going ahead of you to Galilee; there you will see him." This is my message for you.' So they left the tomb quickly with fear and great joy, and ran to tell his disciples." (Matthew 28:1-8)

Encountering the risen Jesus

It is telling that neither of the Marys seemed to be overly frightened by either the earthquake or the angel of the Lord nor did they balk at doing the angel's bidding. I (Victoria) have had the experience of being awakened by an earthquake and I found it completely disorienting not to mention a bit terrifying. My mother and I were visiting my older sister and her husband in Walnut Creek, California, and after staying up late and playing board games, we had all finally settled down to sleep for the night.

I had just drifted off to sleep when suddenly I was awakened by the motion of the bed—it felt like I was lying on a float in the ocean rolling over the waves. It took me a second to realize what had happened and excited voices roused me further. I rushed to the living room where everyone was gathering to hash over what they had experienced. My brother-in-law was still holding his toothbrush as we had all had to share their one bathroom. Fortunately, there were no aftershocks, and we were soon back in bed and sleeping soundly until morning.

While none of us experienced any major revelations or were confronted by an angel that night, it doesn't diminish the fact that God often uses nature to get our attention about something.

Pine Log United Methodist Church near Rydal, Georgia, is a case in point. Both the church and camp are the product of an earthquake that took place in 1866. As we relate in our book, *Touring the Backroads of North and South Georgia*:

"It was August, and the congregation had endured a sweltering week-long series of meetings. The pastor, Reverend

J.N. Sullivan was preaching fervently, but the congregation was just not responding. Finally, Sullivan fell to his knees and prayed, 'Lord, if it takes it to move the hearts of these people, shake the ground on which this old building stands.'

"The words were barely out of Sullivan's mouth before the building shook perceptibly. Even Sullivan's water glass and pitcher, which stood upon the pulpit, shook. The reaction was immediate. People rushed toward the altar to pray. Others heard of the event and rushed from their homes to the church. The worshippers continued to pray that night."

Even after it was learned that what they had experienced were the shock waves from a major earthquake that had occurred in Charleston, South Carolina, the fact that he prayed right before the quake was significant. Sullivan's prayer worked miracles. The congregation was filled with a new religious fervor and Pine Log UMC, and the church continues to prosper.

But revelations from God aren't always so obvious. Like Elijah, we might just hear a "still, small voice" in the form of a flower or a tree. Or, in my case, a dove. I had returned from a visit to the Holocaust Museum in Washington, DC, feeling hopeless and depressed—the age-old question of how a loving God could allow something like that to happen weighing down my heart.

I put my purse down and went into the kitchen to prepare dinner when I noticed a movement out of the corner of my eye. I turned to face the window and there on the ledge outside sat a dove, its round black eye regarding me. It was as if the Holy Spirit was saying: I am with you always.

Encountering the risen Jesus

And I realized that was true—God is always there. In the midst of horror, tragedy, grief, celebration, everything. God is always with us.

Coincidence? Maybe. But I felt in my heart it was a sign of God's love and presence and it was enough to lift me from my depression and experience hope, once again.

As Howard Thurman said, "In any wilderness the unsuspecting traveler may come upon the burning bush and discover that the ground upon which he stands is holy ground."

- When has nature turned your eyes or heart to God?

Landscape with Moses and the Burning Bush by Domenichino (Italian, 1610-1616)

Holy Mysteries
THURSDAY – QUOTATION

Holy Sonnet 10

Death, be not proud, though some have called thee
Mighty and dreadful, for thou art not so;
For those whom thou think'st thou dost overthrow
Die not, poor Death, nor yet canst thou kill me.
From rest and sleep, which but thy pictures be,
Much pleasure; then from thee much more must flow,
And soonest our best men with thee do go,
Rest of their bones, and soul's delivery.
Thou art slave to fate, chance, kings, and desperate men,
And dost with poison, war, and sickness dwell,
And poppy or charms can make us sleep as well
And better than thy stroke; why swellst thou then?
One short sleep past, we wake eternally
And death shall be no more; Death, thou shalt die.

-John Donne (1572–1631), *Holy Sonnets*

John Donne composed the nineteen poems known as the Holy Sonnets in 1609-1610 during a time of great financial and emotional stress. In his preaching as well as his poetry, Donne often returned to death and resurrection as one burdened by past sins who was concerned for the state of his soul. Here he moves from calling personified Death "mighty and dreadful," to noting that Death does not act by his own will, but is driven by the whims of fate and chance as well as people both noble and common. He ends by proclaiming the coming death of Death.

Donne had been born into a Roman Catholic family and saw his brother Henry arrested in 1593 for hiding the Catholic priest William Harrington, who would be martyred the next year. Henry died of bubonic plague while in prison. By the time he wrote the sonnets, Donne was struggling with the idea of converting to the Anglican Church as well as whether to consent to be ordained at King James' urging, which happened in 1615. Donne would rise to become one of the most well-known Anglican priests of the 17th century as the Dean of London's St. Paul's Cathedral from 1621-1631. While he is now lauded as one of the great metaphysical poets, his poems circulated in hand-written manuscripts shared among friends and benefactors. The Holy Sonnets, like much of his work, were not published in his lifetime. We will return to Donne who meditated often on holy mysteries and wrote memorably about death and resurrection.

- What surprises or comforts you in John Donne's sonnet?

Holy Mysteries
Friday – The Linen Wrappings

"Then Peter and the other disciple set out and went towards the tomb. The two were running together, but the other disciple outran Peter and reached the tomb first. He bent down to look in and saw the linen wrappings lying there, but he did not go in. Then Simon Peter came, following him, and went into the tomb. He saw the linen wrappings lying there, and the cloth that had been on Jesus' head, not lying with the linen wrappings but rolled up in a place by itself. Then the other disciple, who reached the tomb first, also went in, and he saw and believed; for as yet they did not understand the scripture, that he must rise from the dead. Then the disciples returned to their homes." (John 20:3-10)

Outpacing Peter in the dash to discover what happened to Jesus, John sees the linen wrappings without pushing into the tomb itself. Peter goes inside and discovers the head cloth rolled up and set in a place by itself. Jesus' resurrection is so different from the scene just over a week earlier when Lazarus came out of the tomb when Jesus ordered the same disciples to unbind Lazarus.

Lazarus' ankles would have been tied together and his wrists bound in front of him. He would have also had a strap around his chin. Then rather than being wrapped mummy-style, there would have been a large burial sheet under the length of his body that in one piece went up his back over his head and down the front. This shroud would have been

Encountering the risen Jesus

The Raising of Lazarus by Lucas von Leyden (c. 1507)

further strapped around in place with wrappings. Lazarus was quite literally bound up in his burial clothes.

In contrast, the disciples who raced to the tomb saw the linen wrappings neatly stacked showing that Jesus is no longer bound by death. This clarity comes to John, yet he still does not fully understand what has happened for we are told both that John also went into the tomb, saw, and believed. John adds, "for as yet they did not understand the scripture, that he must rise from the dead." Perhaps he thinks Jesus has been resuscitated to die again like Lazarus. Or perhaps, he imagines Jesus has returned to his Father.

John's Gospel shows how the light of the glory of what God had done in raising Jesus was slow to dawn on his followers. It takes time for the eyes of their hearts to adjust to the light. With the certainty that he is no longer in his grave, but still lacking clarity of what did occur, Peter and John return home. This is common in John's Gospel as the light does not come to us in its fullness all at once, but there are stages of belief as our faith deepens with new experiences of Jesus. With teaching on the mysteries of the faith in Eastertide, Christian communities made room for further enlightenment.

- What questions of faith do you have where you long for great clarity or confirmation?
- Pray for the Holy Spirit to deepen your faith with new experiences and insight as you continue the journey of Easter.

Encountering the risen Jesus
Saturday – Victoria's Reflection

"The possession of knowledge does not kill
the sense of wonder and mystery.
There is always more mystery."
-Anaïs Nin

My fascination with the mystery of the Shroud of Turin began in December of 1982. My sister and I had accompanied our grandmother to a doctor's appointment in Atlanta, and while she was doing her thing, my sister and I did some Christmas shopping and then met Frank at a Shroud of Turin exhibit located in the Peachtree Center in Atlanta and hosted by Episcopal priest Kim Dreisbach.

At that point I was not at all familiar with The Shroud of Turin. The relic is referred to as being 'of Turin' because the Italian city is the repository for the shroud. The Shroud was, allegedly, the cloth which wrapped Jesus's dead body, the linen wrappings referenced in yesterday's scripture reading in this devotional. What makes the Shroud so special, though, is its central mystery—the body image that is imprinted on it.

In the subtlest tones of yellow sepia one can see on the 14'3" x 3'7" cloth both the back and front of a man as if he had been placed upon it, feet at the bottom, and the top end draped over the front of his body. The top half shows a bearded face, a pronounced chest, hands crossed over the groin, and legs side by side. The bottom bears the imprint of the back of the head with a long rope of hair, taut shoulders and buttocks, and soles of the feet. In addition, on the herringbone-woven linen, one can see blood—on the crown of the head, on the chest, the wrists, the ankles as well as what looks like blood stains from someone being whipped. Even more astounding to me was the fact that when a photograph was taken of the Shroud it was as if the Shroud itself was a negative and an even clearer image appeared to the unaided eye.

There are so many more things one can write about the Shroud; in fact, entire books have been written about it. Suffice to say, its origin has posed a mystery for centuries as it has, ostensibly, been around for nearly 2,000 years. While there is evidence of it being in Turkey—Edessa and Constantinople—for centuries, the Shroud's appearance in Europe, probably appearing first in France, isn't verified until the 14th century.

The Shroud of Turin was so incredibly intriguing to me when I saw the images for the first time in Atlanta: the life-size image of the Shroud and the three-dimensional sculpture made a huge impact. Was this really an image of Jesus? My heart said yes.

Sixteen years later, Frank was finishing up his first year in Seminary and we were visiting my grandmother and mother in Statesboro. It would have been after April 20, 1998, because that is when *Time Magazine* published its cover story on the Shroud of Turin, in which it focused on the 1988 carbon dating proving that the Shroud was a medieval forgery. I saw the magazine at my grandmother's house, read the article, and was deeply disappointed because I had felt so strongly that it was real. Later, I needed a pencil, and I went to my grandfather's room (he died in 1988) to check his desk. In the drawer of his desk, in the hollow area made to hold pens and paper clips, I found two pencils—one, a small red pencil that had Time Magazine printed on it; the other, a white pencil with the names of the books of the New Testament printed on it.

Yes, some might say coincidence but as Dale C. Allison, Jr. writes in his book *Encountering Mystery: Religious Experience in a Secular Age*:

> "James Leuba, the influential psychologist of religion, spoke for a multitude when he ascribed mystical experiences to misapprehension and psychopathology. Skepticism is not confined to the academy. It is also at home in certain religious circles. In many churches and among many seminary-educated pastors there is a far-flung prejudice against metanormal experiences, a predisposition not to take them seriously."

He continues later, "… without a congenial framework for reception, a framework that Catholic theology had supplied, and Protestantism deleted, people stopped recounting their experiences."

I could dismiss the two pencils catching my eye at that time when I wondered about the shroud. Yet the coincidence was so astounding that I took it to be a sign that the science had not gotten it right. I still held that the Shroud of Turin was really the linen wrappings that had covered Jesus. While my faith does not depend on that cloth relic alone, I do see it as a sign of the power of God.

- Have you experienced a coincidence as a God-incident, God using something to get your attention?
- How do you separate these incidents from the genuine coincidences that naturally occur as well?

Sunday – Mystery Revisited

On the Sunday evening following Jesus' death by crucifixion, the disciples are locked in the upper room in Jerusalem where they celebrated the Last Supper (John 20:19-31). They are gathered in fear that the same fate endured by the Rabbi awaits them. Jesus appears among them and says, "Peace be with you." He says, "As the Father has sent me, so I send you" and then breathes on them, literally inspiring them with the gift of the Holy Spirit. On this first Easter, we see God the Father, Son, and Holy Spirit present with Jesus' fearful followers.

We would not conceive of God as a Trinity of persons if this had not been revealed, but having been shown to us we can see how this image of the divine does fit a cosmos where the interconnections among all creation are deeply true. In this sense, the Holy Trinity is not a mystery in any way like a whodunit, where we search for The Answer. God the Father, Son, and Holy Spirit are a mystery in the sense that the more we come to know the more we see there is to be known. There is a truth present in this way of envisioning the Holy One that reveals why humans long for connection–we were created out of love for love. God who was in communion with God's own self before the creation, made us for that type of connection.

The New Testament Greek for this is *koinonia*, which is often translated as "community" or "fellowship." *Koinonia* is a close connection. To have *koinonia* with something or someone is to participate with it and in it. A better translation for *koinonia* is communion and our communion service is called just that because in communion we have and celebrate *koinonia* with God and with each other.

In the Eucharist, we participate in the very life of God. The Holy Mystery of the sacrament Jesus instituted on the night before he died has depths we cannot fully fathom.

Physicists emphasize "spacetime" as unified rather than there being "space" that we experience over "time." The math reveals space and time as one, all of space and time are interconnected. The distinction between my participating in the Eucharist celebrated for diocesan staff in our office chapel with seven of us present and my participating in the Archbishop of Canterbury celebrating the Eucharist for the more than 650 bishops of the Anglican Communion is less important than the connection between them. Each time you participate in the Eucharist you are connected to all the other people receiving communion around the world on that same day. You are also connected to all the times in which the Eucharist has been celebrated, from those preparing for martyrdom in a Roman Coliseum to your beloved great-grandmother receiving the sacrament hours before her death.

Holy Mysteries

Time is held within eternity. The ineffable connection that was present in the Holy Trinity before creation, inhabits all of spacetime, and is with us always. This is not a mystery to solve and while we can experience it, we can ever fully explain it.

Like the Nordic Noir detective moving at a glacial pace to learn more, we too can continue past the set answers to find more questions to pursue, more mystery to sit with as we see the truth in this way of conceiving of life, the universe, and everything even as we know there is more to discover. The heart of God is not unknown and unknowable, so much as something we see through a glass darkly, knowing that there will continue to be hidden depths in which we discover more throughout our lives. All of the mysteries of the faith the early church taught in the season between Easter and Pentecost fall into this category of being well-known and never fully comprehended.

- Have you ever felt a strong connection to someone who was far away, such as suddenly feeling the need to pray for someone for no identifiable reason?
- How has your experience and understanding of participating in the Holy Eucharist changed over time?

Week II
Water

Monday – Introducing Water

"John the baptizer appeared in the wilderness,
proclaiming a baptism of repentance
for the forgiveness of sins."
~Mark 1:4

The untamable prophet, John, stands in the water of the Jordan River calling his people to turn back to God. His message is as coarse as his clothes, yet people flock to the wilderness to hear him preach. They responded to his call in a ritual that was not wholly new. To the Jews jostling in line on Jordan's banks in response to the Baptist's cry, the act of immersion would have brought to mind a *mikveh* where the practice of washing represented spiritual cleansing. The *mikveh* was a bath specially built for observing the Torah's commands related to ritual washing, from a woman who completed her menstrual cycle or a person who touched a corpse to someone preparing to visit the Temple in Jerusalem or for the consecration of a priest. In the century before Jesus, purpose-built *mikvehs* were increasingly common. Prior to that time, the rite took place in nature similar to John's ritual bathing in the Jordan, which he says is a baptism of repentance for the forgiveness of sins.

The ritual cleansing in Holy Baptism pushes this further. Notice how the Book of Common Prayer uses death to describe the water of Baptism:

> In it we are buried with Christ in his death.
> By it we share in his resurrection.
> Through it we are reborn by the Holy Spirit.

Baptism is not so much merely ritual cleansing as ritual drowning. While this could sound extreme, scripture says we are united with Jesus through baptism to his death and through that connection to his resurrection. So rather than cleansing, which needs to happen again and again, baptism is death and rebirth, which only happens once. Baptism is the one-time act, through which we become members of Christ's Body, the church.

We may later err, but we remain God's child and members of Christ's Body. When we make mistakes, we are to repent and return to the Lord, asking forgiveness as we seek to amend our lives. This then becomes the shape of the Christian life: We commit ourselves to God, go out to live a more Christ-like life. We then fall short of the mark set by God. We notice the sin in our lives, and we return to God asking for forgiveness again. In time, we are to conform our lives more and more to Christ.

Encountering the risen Jesus

Noah's Ark has long been connected to Christian baptism. Carvings of the Ark were a common decoration for baptismal fonts for centuries. The reason is that those who got into the Ark were saved through water, as Peter puts it in a New Testament letter. Peter writes that it is not something comparable to cleansing from dirt that baptism offers, because through baptism we find not just a one time forgiveness of sins, but a new birth to an ongoing connection to God. So, the connection goes, as all who got into the Ark found salvation, so all who pass through the waters of baptism find salvation and entrance into the great Ark of the church.

This image highlights how baptism is a chance to firmly establish your commitment, not just to God but to the rest of the faithful. For Jesus taught that we are not just to love God, but also to love our neighbors as ourselves. Christianity is a community endeavor. Baptism always has both an individual and a communal aspect. We tend to stress the individual part, while almost forgetting that baptism is not just an event in the life of a family. Baptism is always also an event in the life of a community of faith.

The community of faith then is where we work on the second part of what we see in Jesus' baptism. What happened next was the Spirit guiding Jesus into the wilderness for forty days of fasting and prayer before he began his ministry. Jesus' faithfulness in baptism is followed by him faithfully spending time alone in prayer. God who creates and recreates longs not for our doing as much as our being. And in being with God, much change can follow over time as we are part of a church. This two-fold action is described by two fifty-cent words used in theology—justification and sanctification—which work like pop-tarts and pickles.

A pop-tart has its moment to shine when the toaster pops it up once it has been heated enough. Something was going on in the toaster, and then the moment arrived and out popped the tart. It is now done, now warm and ready to eat. This is like baptism, in that the Spirit will have been working in one's soul to bring them to the baptismal waters and then in baptism, pop, in a moment it is done. One baptism for all time. Done.

Then there are pickles. There is the preparation of a mixture of vinegar, salt, spices, and sometimes sugar, which is brought to a boil and then poured over cucumbers packed into clean glass jars. What follows takes time for the cucumber to become the pickle as it continues to marinate in the mixture.

Justification is a pop-tart, as it can happen in a moment. Put your trust in God and God sees you as justified, not because you are perfect, but because you are perfectly loved by the God who made you and wants to be with you always. The pickle is sanctification, the process of becoming more and more holy, more and more Christ-like. This is the work that takes time.

Here the image of water is most helpful. Like a mountain stream that takes the rough edges off the rocks as it pours across them year after year, so with time, God works in my soul. Only in looking back at the difference over time, can I see the ways in which my mind and more importantly my heart have been transformed by the love of God as found in Jesus. Our baptisms were a one time act, but through the means of grace we nourish the lifelong process of sanctification. Means of grace is an expression for how the sacraments (especially the Eucharist), prayers, and good works, assist us in our faith journey. Some of this, like prayer, we can do alone, but most of the means of grace require other people. To become more and more like Jesus, we need not only God, but we also need Christ's body, the Church, into which we were initiated in the water of baptism.

- What do you know about your own baptism? What other baptisms have you found it meaningful to watch or take part in?
- What ways has your faith changed you over time that people around you might notice?

Holy Mysteries
Tuesday – Victoria's Reflection

> "God is trying to sell you something,
> but you don't want to buy.
> This is what your suffering is:
> Your fantastic haggling,
> your manic screaming over the price!"
>
> ~Hafiz on dying to the False Self

In the autumn of 2022, I decided to take a class offered by the Center for Action and Contemplation started by Franciscan Richard Rohr. The class was called "Immortal Diamond" and was based on Rohr's book of the same name. Essentially, the book is about realizing that your "False Self" is just that and working toward revealing one's "True Self"—The Immortal Diamond.

As Rohr writes, "Our True Self is surely the 'treasure hidden in the field' that Jesus speaks of. It is your own chunk of the immortal diamond. He says that we should 'happily be willing to sell everything to buy that field' (Matthew 13:44)—or that diamond mine! ... In all the Gospels, Jesus is quoted as saying, 'What will it profit you if you gain the whole world and lose your own soul?' (Matthew 16:26) ... It is indeed the 'pearl of great price' (Matthew 13:46)."

But to find that treasure hidden in a field one must come to terms with one's "False Self" and realize that aspect of you is not what God sees and loves.

"Your False Self," Rohr writes, "which we might also call

your 'small self,' is your launching pad: your body image, your job, your education, your clothes, your money, your car, your sexual identity, your success, and so on."

So, in essence, my "False Self" is the self that I project to all those I meet. As I progressed through the class, I came to realize that my "False Self" is my "what will they think?" self. What will they think if I say X? What will they think if I wear X? What will they think if . . .? And that, honestly, is one of the most difficult things to let go of. But God gave me a chance to do so. On January 14, 2023, to be exact.

On that day, I received an email asking me if I would consider being the keynote speaker at the meeting for the Southeast Convocation of the Third Order, Society of Saint Francis (TSSF) in the spring of 2024. We hadn't had one of these annual meetings since before Covid and it was time to start again. My first reaction was fear and panic, but after a few deep breaths, I realized that the least I could do was pray about it and see if God was leading me toward doing this.

After prayerful consideration, I felt that God was indeed calling me toward doing something I had never done before. Public speaking is not my forte but with a year's notice, I felt sure I would be able to come up with three talks. I knew that Frank and I would be attending the TSSF Provincial Convocation in Scottsdale, Arizona, that year because it fell just a couple of days after our daughter's graduation from vet school in Phoenix. I thought that I might be able to take some of the themes from that meeting and carry them forward to our convocation meeting the next spring.

And as wonderful as that was, including hearing our

keynote speaker, Ilia Delio, OSF, PhD, a Franciscan Sister of Washington, DC, and an American theologian specializing in the area of science and religion, with interests in evolution, physics, and neuroscience, and the import of these for theology, that is not where I found my inspiration. No, it was in our small group discussions that I began to reflect on humility, love, and joy which are the three notes of our Order.

I continued to reflect on these once I was home again and began to consider daily: 1) something that had happened during the past 24 hours that kept me humble; 2) something I had done in the past 24 hours out of love; and 3) something that had brought me joy in the past 24 hours.

By December, with the convocation retreat now scheduled for mid-April, I made a promise to myself to write one talk a month in January, February, and March, and then familiarize myself with them, knowing as I did so that I planned to speak from my script as I was not practiced at public speaking.

The only thing left to overcome was my stage fright at speaking publicly! And that's when I realized I needed to take "Immortal Diamond" to heart.

As Richard Rohr notes, "In the most mature stage of spiritual development, I'm 'just me,' warts and all. We are now fully detached from our own self-image and living in God's image of us—which includes and loves both the good and the bad. We experience true serenity and freedom. This is the peace the world cannot give (see John 14:27) and full resting in God."

Encountering the risen Jesus

Victoria addresses the diocesan convention in 2023 as the President of Episcopal Youth and Children Services.

I needed to not care what anyone in person or watching via Zoom thought of me. I had worked on my talks and Frank had assured me I had something to say. I didn't matter. What I had to say mattered. Because, as Franciscans, humility, love, and joy should be at the very heart of who we are. And it worked! I was only a little nervous but not enough to keep me from speaking. I made mistakes—mixed words, lost my place, had to deal with a rough voice a few times—but I was also able to ad lib some as well, and all in all I think it went pretty well.

Best of all, having done that successfully, I have been able to speak more confidently in my positions as Chair of the Episcopal Youth and Children's Services board as well as interact and speak to the spouses of Bishops as a board member of the Spouse Planning Group (planning events for spouses at General Convention and House of Bishops meetings). I'm not 100% at public speaking now and probably never will be, and that's fine.

But I hope I am closer to worrying less about my "False Self" and concentrating more on my "True Self" because as Richard Rohr says in *Immortal Diamond*: "If all you have at the end of your life is your False Self, there will not be much to eternalize. It is transitory. … Your False Self is what changes, passes, and dies when you die. Only your True Self lives forever."

- Can you separate your False Self from your True Self? What aspect of your False Self bothers you the most?
- Have you ever allowed your True Self to shine or are you afraid of what others will think if you let them see the real you?

Wednesday – The Gardener

"But Mary stood weeping outside the tomb. As she wept, she bent over to look into the tomb; and she saw two angels in white, sitting where the body of Jesus had been lying, one at the head and the other at the feet. They said to her, 'Woman, why are you weeping?' She said to them, 'They have taken away my Lord, and I do not know where they have laid him.' When she had said this, she turned round and saw Jesus standing there, but she did not know that it was Jesus. Jesus said to her, 'Woman, why are you weeping? For whom are

Encountering the risen Jesus

you looking?' Supposing him to be the gardener, she said to him, 'Sir, if you have carried him away, tell me where you have laid him, and I will take him away.'" (John 20:11-15)

Far from a simple case of mistaken identity, Mary Magdalene closely aligned to the truth when she thought the man was the gardener. Given that she knew Jesus to be dead, her error made sense. But we do well to attend to the dramatic irony in this detail. Mary Magdalene thought this momentary lapse was worth retelling or we would not know of this story of mistaken identity. The author of the Gospel also knew that this was too important to leave out of the story. John's Gospel starts with the words, "In the beginning" then as Jesus is crucified we get the detail, "The place of crucifixion was near a garden, where there was a new tomb, never used before" (John 19:41). We know that John's Gospel is well aware of how Jesus' life and ministry connect back to the beginning.

The Incarnation, God becoming human in Jesus, was the crucial part of a project undertaken to bring creation back to the Garden of Eden. Jesus' death and resurrection are the final stages in his defeat of death itself. At the culmination of this long project, working its way through all human history, Mary Magdalene sees Jesus as the gardener. In this mistake, Mary sees most clearly. For Jesus was not a teacher who was mistaken for a gardener, but a gardener who was mistaken to be merely a teacher.

Jesus certainly was a great teacher, but not through

teaching Seven Spiritual Laws, or any other teaching to be mastered by memorization. Jesus was a teacher primarily in living among us a life of grace and love and forgiveness and in so doing showed us how to live. While Jesus would condense his teaching to "Love the Lord your God with all your heart, mind, soul and strength and Love your neighbor as yourself" it was in the way he lived this out that we gained the clearest picture of what he meant by that teaching. Jesus taught through his actions and so in that way his very life plants and tends the Kingdom of God within us. Jesus came to work the soil in our hardened hearts, to help spark spiritual growth in the depths of our souls. Jesus came to offer the loving care that a gardener gives to that beloved prize-winning plant that is the centerpiece of the garden. That plant is you. The story of Easter is that the gardener did all he did in order for you to bear much fruit.

- Who have you known or who have you read about whose lives could be said to bear much fruit?

Thursday – Quotation

"I have long been wishing, O true-born and dearly beloved children of the Church, to discourse to you concerning these spiritual and heavenly Mysteries; but since I well knew that seeing is far more persuasive than hearing, I waited for the present season; that finding you more open to the influence of my words from your present experience, I might lead you by the hand into the brighter and more fragrant meadow of the Paradise before us; especially as ye have been made fit to receive the more sacred Mysteries, after having been found worthy of divine and life-giving Baptism. Since therefore it remains to set before you a table of the more perfect instructions, let us now teach you these things exactly, that ye may know the effect wrought upon you on that evening of your baptism." (Cyril of Jerusalem's Lecture 19: *On the Mysteries I*)

"Let no one then suppose that Baptism is merely the grace of remission of sins, or further, that of adoption; as John's was a baptism conferring only remission of sins: whereas we know full well, that as it purges our sins, and ministers to us the gift of the Holy Ghost, so also it is the counterpart of the sufferings of Christ. For this cause Paul just now cried aloud and said, 'Or are ye ignorant that all we who were baptized into Christ Jesus, were baptized into His death? We were buried therefore with Him by baptism into His death.' These words he spoke to some who were disposed to think that Baptism ministers to us the remission of sins, and adoption, but has not furthered the fellowship also, by representation, of Christ's true sufferings.

"In order therefore that we might learn, that whatsoever things Christ endured, 'for us and for our salvation.' He suffered them in reality and not in appearance, and that we also are made partakers of His sufferings, Paul cried with all exactness of truth, For if we have been planted together with the likeness of His death, we shall be also with the likeness of His resurrection. Well has he said, planted together. For since the true Vine was planted in this place, we also by partaking in the Baptism of death have been planted together with Him. And fix thy mind with much attention on the words of the Apostle. He said not, 'For if we have been planted together with His death,' but, with the likeness of His death. For in Christ's case there was death in reality, for His soul was really separated from His body, and real burial, for His holy body was wrapt in pure linen; and everything happened really to Him; but in your case there was only a likeness of death and sufferings, whereas of salvation there was not a likeness but a reality." (Cyril of Jerusalem's Lecture 20: *On the Mysteries II*)

In his first and second lectures on the Holy Mysteries, Cyril of Jerusalem opens up the meaning of the baptism just experienced by those he is teaching in the church that is believed to encompass the sites of Jesus' death and resurrection. Cyril connects baptism to Jesus teaching on the night before he died, "I am the vine, you are the branches. Those who abide in me and I in them bear much fruit, because apart from me you can do nothing." He names that the true Vine was planted in this place, and in baptism we are planted together with him. Our baptisms do affect the forgiveness of sins and adoption as joint heirs with Christ. Baptism also unites us with Jesus in his passion and resurrection. As Paul wrote, 'For if we have been united with him in a death like his, we will certainly be united with him in a resurrection like his" (Romans 6.5).

- If your child, niece or nephew, grandchild or Godchild asked what happens in baptism, how would you describe to them its meaning?

FRIDAY – FRANK'S REFLECTION

I know that baptism is supposed to be a once and for all time event and yet that hasn't been my personal experience as I have been baptized twice.

I was first baptized as an infant at First United Methodist Church in Montgomery, Alabama. Promises were made and water was splashed on my head as I was baptized in the name of the Father, Son, and Holy Spirit. The heavens did not break open. The Holy Spirit may have indeed descended, but certainly not like a dove. And there was no voice from heaven. However, during the first six years of my life, spent in that Methodist Church on Cloverdale Park, I did come to believe quite sincerely that the Rev. Dr. Joel McDavid, the minister who baptized me, was God and that his assistant was Jesus. And so I did feel like I heard God speak in that church on many occasions.

Ten years later I was in baptismal waters again. This time I stepped down into the baptistery behind the choir loft at Mount Paran Church of God in Atlanta. My whole family took turns being fully immersed by the Rev. Dr. Paul Walker. I remember bobbing along on tip toes to keep my head fully out of the water. Once again, the heavens didn't open and there were no really notable special effects. But we did note

Holy Mysteries

that my Dad's rather bad cold was healed on the spot.

Another 21 years passed. This time I was 31 years old and I stepped forward at St. Peter's Episcopal Church to reaffirm publicly my faith in Jesus Christ and to confirm the promises of baptism. There was no water this time, but the laying on of hands by the Rt. Rev. Frank Allan, Bishop of the Diocese of Atlanta. I know many people have said that confirmation was not particularly meaningful for them and in nine years of attending Episcopal Churches, I had not previously found cause to be confirmed. Yet, while there were no special effects involved, as I renewed my faith first proclaimed for me in my baptism as an infant, I did really feel the Holy Spirit's presence in that service.

In the 31 years since my confirmation, I have attended a number of baptisms including those where I served as a Godparent and the 118 baptisms I celebrated as a priest in the first decade of King of Peace in Kingsland, as well as those I have since officiated as a Canon and now as Bishop. Rather than a once and for all time event, I seem to keep working my way back to the font and the waters of baptism.

When I was confirmed at St. Peter's, the rector, Don Black, challenged me to get a spiritual director to assist me in creating a Rule of Life. This was all new to me. I learned to pray the Daily Offices of Morning and Evening Prayer and so found a consistent rhythm for the spirituality that spoke deeply to me. I learned about a variety of spiritual practices from prayer beads to the labyrinth and centering prayer to Lectio Divina. In the process, I found myself connected not to a static church, but a place of pilgrimage, a place where we were challenged to a journey of faith. This was step two of the two-fold justification and sanctification we find in the Holy Mysteries, we are initiated into the Body of Christ as the beginning of an ongoing journey.

In being connected to a church, I have experienced people showing me not how I needed to change and be different as much as helping me become more fully myself. Perhaps that shouldn't be surprising as others often see things within us we have trouble seeing with the same clarity. Put another way, we all struggle our whole lives to learn a few things about ourselves that a complete stranger could tell us within fifteen minutes. As bishop, I am not past this, but have more to face in this role.

As Victoria wrote, becoming more Christ-like means shedding the illusions of our false self, the self that is fueled by egocentric drives. The false self is the version driven by shame and fear, even though we rarely glimpse this is what drives us. I know that the wounded child of God who is Frank, can allow Bishop Logue (a false self if ever there was one) to work tirelessly at being smart enough, wise enough, holy enough while missing that behind the façade of my social media feed, which is a true reflection of part of my life, there is the very real, imperfect Frank, who I don't have to hide. That broken guy is the one God loves. That true self is actually enough. In fact, any self-perfected, over inflated, version of myself is someone God does not recognize and within whom the Holy Spirit has no room to move toward healing and wholeness.

I get the opportunity to reflect on how I am doing at

Holy Mysteries

A photo of me with Zeke, Jonna, and Gabe Taylor after Zeke's baptism in 2022 in the same font at King of Peace in which I baptized Jonna on Easter in 2001.

living into my baptismal vows many more weeks than most Episcopalians as the majority of visitations to a congregation include renewing our baptismal covenant. I recite the Apostles' Creed and then answer five questions which ask if

Encountering the risen Jesus

I will continue in the same teaching, fellowship, corporate worship and private prayers that sustained the first followers of Jesus; persevere in resisting evil, and, whenever I fall into sin, repent and return to the Lord; as I proclaim by word and example the Good News of God in Christ; seek and serve Christ in all persons; and strive for justice and peace among all people, respecting the dignity of every human being.

Safely ensconced in the ark of the church, I revisit these promises made in baptism, and in the process, I am brought to consider how I am living these noble ideals out in the busyness of my life. Writing reflections like the ones Victoria and I offer in this book, *Holy Mysteries*, is a way to consider this further: how is my faith in Jesus changing me over time like the cold, clear water of a creek rushing over rough stones. When I am honest, I can see some rough spots yet to go as I need to let go of past hurts and even recent incidents that wounded me, where I need to offer grace and forgiveness to someone else and to receive it for myself. While my two baptisms and one confirmation are quite sufficient, the ongoing process of dying to myself continues.

- What spiritual practices such as praying the offices or contemplative prayer have you found fruitful?
- Where do you see rough spots that still need more of the water of the Spirit to wash over them?

SATURDAY – APOSTLE TO THE APOSTLES

"Jesus said to her, 'Mary!' She turned and said to him in Hebrew, 'Rabbouni!' (which means Teacher). Jesus said to her, 'Do not hold on to me, because I have not yet ascended to the Father. But go to my brothers and say to them, "I am ascending to my Father and your Father, to my God and your God."' Mary Magdalene went and announced to the disciples, 'I have seen the Lord'; and she told them that he had said these things to her." (John 20:16-18)

With the certainty that he is no longer in his grave, but still lacking clarity of what did occur, Peter and John have already returned to the upper room where they had celebrated the Passover. Only Mary Magdalene remains. She stands weeping outside the tomb. As she weeps, she bends over to look in the tomb to find angels sitting where Jesus' body had lain in repose, one at the head, the other at the foot. The stone rolled away from the tomb made her fearful and the angels did not bring clarity.

Then she turns and she fails to recognize Jesus who asks her "Woman, why are you weeping? Whom are you looking for?" After mistaking him for the gardener, the Magdalena remains confused. She cannot grasp the world-changing revelation of Jesus' resurrection. Then Jesus said to her one word, "Mary" and nothing will ever be the same again. When he calls her by name, Mary Magdalene understands that this is truly her teacher. Jesus has risen from the grave to never die again.

Encountering the risen Jesus

Hearing her name called by Jesus, the light of the glory of God floods in. The one who went out that early morning into the darkness of the night has returned enlightened by the risen Jesus. She goes to the disciples still locked away in the upper room telling them, "I have seen the Lord." Mary Magdalene becomes the Apostle to the Apostles, bringing them the Good News that life has conquered death. More appearances will follow and they are needed to convince the others, but from the moment Jesus called her name, Mary Magdalene understood that her teacher, who had been truly dead, was risen to new life.

- Why was it so difficult for his followers to understand that Jesus had been resurrected?
- Why did saying her name make the difference?

Sunday – Water Revisited

The Apostle Paul tells us that we are united with Jesus through baptism to his death and through that connection to his resurrection. So rather than cleansing, which needs to happen again and again, baptism is death and rebirth, which only happens once. We may later err, but we remain God's children and members of Christ's Body. When we make mistakes, we then repent and return to God asking forgiveness as we pledge to change and not commit that same sin again. This then becomes the shape of the Christian life as we commit ourselves to God, go out and try to live a more Christ-like life. We then fall short of the mark set by God. We notice the sin in our lives and we return to God asking for forgiveness again.

If we get this wrong, it becomes like an eternally at-the-ready Get-Out-of-Jail-Free card and we ask for forgiveness while intending to do the same thing again. Obviously, this is not true repentance and the only person you kid in this case is yourself. But when you genuinely regret what you have done wrong, and genuinely desire to make a change, then God recognizes that and continually holds out forgiveness as you seek to amend your life and try to conform more and more to being the person God made you to be.

The truth is that no matter how genuine your conversion and your desire to live like Jesus, some will still be prone to gossip, judging others, and losing their temper and saying things they shouldn't say. Others will want to live Christ-like lives and then find themselves locked in abusing drugs, stealing, or committing adultery. It's a fact that people who have genuinely committed themselves to God in baptism have gone on to do some very bad things. And it is true, that those who have done so can genuinely repent, change from doing wrong, separate themselves from the past and become new people once again. In doing so, they will find God's forgiveness and will have no need to be baptized again. The emphasis in this week of reflections has therefore leaned toward practices of faith that are aimed at our ongoing sanctification so we don't have to get into those deep waters. While we won't arrive at anything near perfection, we can make our way to a place where we can ride out the storms of life a little easier because of our faith as we understand at a deep level that God has got us, so we have got what we need for what we are facing.

In his Catechetical Lectures, Cyril connected baptism to Jesus' teaching on the night before he died, "I am the vine, you are the branches." This fits, of course, as we are baptized into Christ's Body, the Church, which grafts us into the vine. Jesus first taught this when he knew his time was short as some of his closest followers would soon scatter into the darkness out of fear when the arrest party arrived. And in those last minutes before his passion, he offered this image of the closest possible connection, telling them that as part of the Body of Christ, we would be as connected to him as branches are to the vine. And if we abide in him, some of the fruit we bear is a peace beyond the present circumstances.

Jesus told the disciples to "abide" which is a word we don't use anymore outside of the church with one helpful exception. In the Coen Brothers' movie "The Big Lebowski", the line "The Dude Abides" is part of the ethos of taking it easy that the main character embodies in the film. Abide means to stay, remain, or rest. Jesus wanted that sort of easy-going connection for us. The Dude in the movie remains unfazed by all that happens in the film. We are taught by watching movies to expect a character arc where the protagonist is changed by all that happens, while we see Jeff Bridges staying so very much himself from start to finish. This is not a bad picture of abiding. We too are to be able to let a lot wash over us as we know that in whatever we face, God will never leave or forsake us. This is not to say

Holy Mysteries

Original art of the characters from The Big Lebowski *created by Grendel Sagrav. Used with permission. All rights reserved.*

that Christians are always too blessed to be stressed or that a follower of Jesus does not worry, but that we need not fall into fear as if we are a people without hope. We can abide because we have already died and been reborn in baptism. What can mortals do to us?

- Have you known someone whose faith sustained them in times that would have sunk someone else?

Week III
Feast

Monday – Introducing Feast

"I am the living bread that came down from heaven.
Whoever eats of this bread will live forever;
and the bread that I will give
for the life of the world is my flesh."

-John 6:51

Even as Jesus is saying these words you can imagine some would-be disciples slipping to the back of the crowd before making a beeline home. Watching Jesus give sight to someone born blind and healing leprosy would have been amazing, but now he is not making any sense. After Jesus says these words, John's Gospel notes that many of his disciples said, "This teaching is difficult; who can accept it?"

The twelve will stick with Jesus, but many others will fall away. Knowing Jesus as a great teacher is one thing, but talking about your flesh as food and your blood as drink must have sounded like the rabbi had lost it. We are so accustomed to speaking of Christ's body and blood in this way, that we could miss the shock of what it was like to hear this when Jesus was still alive. This lengthy bread discourse in the fourth Gospel follows Jesus feeding 5,000 people as the time for the Passover approaches. With that central Jewish feast in mind, Jesus referring to the bread that comes down from heaven makes more sense. Jesus reinterprets the story of the Passover and the Exodus through his own life and ministry.

This week, the theme of Feast follows the lead of Cyril of Jerusalem who used two of his five lectures to explore the holy mystery of the Eucharist. Jesus' miracle of feeding the multitudes as well as his reinterpreting the Passover are central to our understanding of the Eucharistic Feast.

In feeding the 5,000, Jesus has given them physical food, a feast in the wilderness, and then uses that meal to teach that he can give them spiritual food as well. He said, "Do not work for the food that perishes, but for the food that endures for eternal life." He wants those who are listening to him to not just eat some bread and fish and then go home to hunger again. He wants them to develop a spiritual hunger and thirst that he and only he can fill. And to teach this, Jesus uses the Passover story, which was about moving from slavery into freedom to show how faith in him also moves his followers from death to life.

These words from this Gospel, "the bread that I will give for the life of the world is my flesh," are given in the first year of Jesus' three years of ministry. John's Gospel, with these Bread of Life passages coming so early in his ministry, makes clear that the Eucharist is not about Jesus' sacrificial death alone. Our faith is grounded in the Incarnation–Jesus' whole life from Bethlehem to Golgotha and beyond to an empty tomb in a garden, appearances to his disciples, and ascension. Everything Jesus did—who Jesus was and how he acted—are part of God's revelation to us. We are to take Jesus whole story and make it part of our story. God took Jesus' whole life, blessed, broke it, and gave it to us. We are to let that story of God's love for us take us, bless us, break us and give us back to the world.

Dom Gregory Dix in his work of scholarship on the Eucharist, *The Shape of the Liturgy*, wrote, "At the heart of it all is the Eucharistic action, a thing of an absolute simplicity—the taking, blessing, breaking and giving of bread and the taking, blessing and giving of a cup of wine and water, as they were first done with their new meaning by a young Jew before and after supper with His friends on the night before he died….Was ever another command so obeyed? For century after century, spreading slowly to every continent and country and among every race on earth, this action has been done, in every conceivable human circumstance, for every human need from infancy and before it to extreme old age and after it, from the pinnacles of earthly greatness to the refuge of fugitives in the caves and dens of the earth."

We need this strengthening of the Body and Blood of Jesus encountered in the Eucharist as apart from God, we find it easier and easier to remain apart from God and to rely on other, lesser answers to our deep hungers and thirsts which only Jesus can satisfy. This is where the comparison to

Holy Mysteries

physical hunger and thirst helps us as we know that we need the nourishment of food and drink again and again. We may feast now, but we will still need to eat tomorrow and another meal in between those two as well. In that same way we need spiritual nourishment again and again.

From time to time, each of us can find ourselves feeling distanced from God. And so this is word to the wise that when that happens, know that staying away from the altar is not the path to healing and wholeness. Keep going to church. God can handle your doubts and even your anger. Keep asking for and expecting the peace which Jesus alone can give. You need the nourishment you find at the altar as much as you need something to eat and something to drink. It is returning again and again week after week for Jesus' presence in Word and the sacrament of the Eucharist that we are fed. Jesus gave us this bread so that we might live. And in those times in life when challenges rise and we are not sure we have what it takes, we return again to be sustained by Jesus' presence. And if we begin to feel unworthy of God's love, we know that we are still invited to the feast. We can always return to the altar, confess, and receive forgiveness. Then through Christ's presence in the Eucharistic Feast, we are nourished for the days ahead.

- When have you found receiving the Eucharist particularly meaningful?
- If you have found yourself away from church for a time, what brought you back?

Encountering the risen Jesus

TUESDAY – VICTORIA'S REFLECTION

"Fasting and feasting are universal human responses, and any meal, shared with love, can be an agape."

-Elise M. Boulding

When I was much younger, I was perturbed by the term "Eucharistic Feast" because it didn't fit my definition of what I thought a 'feast' was supposed to encompass. How could a wafer and a sip of wine be termed a 'feast'? A feast is supposed to be composed of even more food options than Thanksgiving plus entertainment of some sort. Obviously, my definition of feast was drawn from all the Merlin and King Arthur books I read! Now that I am older and wiser, I understand just how much is contained within that word.

Artificial Intelligence (A.I.) tells me (in 13.5-point Roboto font, which seems apropos) that the Eucharistic Feast is: "a banquet feast that is both a sacrifice and a meal that takes place at an altar. The Eucharist is a memorial of the sacrifice of Christ, who offered his Body and Blood on the cross, and is also a sign of unity, charity, and a paschal banquet."

So, if the Eucharistic Feast is communion within a community, a celebratory feast is people eating together in community, and hopefully, seeking communion with each other. One of my favorite movies is an excellent example of this. Based on the 1958 story of the same name by Isak Dinesen (the pen name of Karen Blixen), "Babette's Feast" is, like most movies, complicated.

The movie is about two sisters, Martine and Filippa, who are elderly and pious Protestants, that live in a small village on the remote western coast of Jutland in 19th-century Denmark. Their late father was a pastor who founded his own Pietistic church, and the sisters now minister to an ever-dwindling congregation.

Forty-nine years earlier, the sisters spurned their suitors in order to remain with their father. Martine turns down a young Swedish cavalry officer, Lorens Löwenhielm, and Filippa rejects the famous baritone Achille Papin, from the Paris Opera.

Thirty-five years later, Babette Hersant appears at their door carrying a letter from Papin explaining that she is a refugee from counter-revolutionary bloodshed in Paris and recommending her as a housekeeper. The sisters cannot afford to employ her, but Babette begs to work for free. For the next 14 years, she serves as their cook, creating improved versions of the bland meals they and the congregation are accustomed to and gaining their respect, and that of the other locals.

Babette's only link to her former life is a lottery ticket that a Parisian friend renews for her annually. One day, she wins the lottery and receives 10,000 francs. After her win she decides to prepare a dinner for the sisters and their small congregation on the occasion of the founding pastor's hundredth birthday. More than just a feast, the meal is also an act of self-sacrifice.

The sisters accept Babette's offer to pay for the creation

of a "real French dinner." Babette arranges for her nephew to go to Paris and gather the supplies for the feast. The ingredients are plentiful and exotic, and their arrival causes a lot of discussion among the villagers. As the various never-before-seen ingredients arrive and preparations commence, the sisters and their congregation begin to worry that the meal will become a sin of sensual luxury, but agree to eat the meal, on the condition they don't take any pleasure in it nor make any mention of the food during the dinner.

Löwenhielm, now a famous general married to a member of the Queen's court, comes as the guest of his aunt, a member of the old pastor's congregation. Unaware of the other guests' plan, not to mention that he was a former attaché in Paris, he is the only person at the table qualified to comment on the meal and does so. He regales the guests with information about the extraordinary food and drink, comparing it to a meal he enjoyed years earlier at the famous Café Anglais in Paris. Although the other guests refuse to comment, Babette's meal breaks down their distrust and superstitions—old wrongs are forgiven while old loves are rekindled, and an almost mystical redemption of the human spirit settles over the table.

The sisters assume that Babette will now return to Paris, but she informs them that all of her money is gone and that she is not going anywhere. She then reveals that she is the former head chef of the Café Anglais, where a dinner for twelve cost 10,000 francs. When Martine cries, "Now you will be poor the rest of your life," Babette replies, "An artist is never poor." Filippa says, "But this is not the end, Babette.

In paradise you will be the great artist God meant you to be." She then embraces her with tears in her eyes saying, "Oh, how you will enchant the angels!"

The movie is both secular and religious and speaks to what John Stott said:

> "The Christian community is a community of the cross, for it has been brought into being by the cross, and the focus of its worship is the Lamb once slain, now glorified. So the community of the cross is a community of celebration, a eucharistic community, ceaselessly offering to God through Christ the sacrifice of our praise and thanksgiving. The Christian life is an unending festival. And the festival we keep, now that our Passover Lamb has been sacrificed for us, is a joyful celebration of his sacrifice, together with a spiritual feasting upon it."

We had the chance to experience an agape meal when we were in Israel. Our group, which was in Israel to explore both the Palestinian and Israeli sides of the story, traveled one day to Hebron, a Palestinian city in the southern West Bank, south of Jerusalem. The third-largest of the Palestinian territories, it had a population of 201,063 Palestinians in 2017 (the year before our trip). There are also 700 or so Jewish settlers concentrated on the outskirts of its Old City. Although the city has been under the civil control of the Palestinian Authority since 1997, the Israeli military maintains a presence in an area comprising 20 percent of the city.

Encountering the risen Jesus

Our host flips the pot containing the maqluba onto the tray for serving the meal Victoria describes in her reflection.

Hebron includes the Cave of the Patriarchs and is considered one of the oldest cities in the country. According to the Bible, Abraham settled in Hebron and bought the Cave of the Patriarchs as a burial place for his wife Sarah. Biblical tradition holds that the patriarchs Abraham, Isaac, and Jacob, along with their wives Sarah, Rebecca, and Leah, were buried in the cave. It was an almost surreal experience to be standing in that ancient place knowing its history while it was watched over by an Orthodox Jew from New York who had settled in the area.

Our group, thirteen of us, were invited to a Palestinian couple's home for lunch and conversation. I honestly don't remember if they were Christian or Muslim, but I do remember their generous hospitality. They prepared a traditional Palestinian meal for us called maqluba, concocted of cauliflower, onion, chicken and rice that are layered in a pot and overturned onto a tray when finished. It is then served with yogurt, slivered almonds, and parsley.

We learned a lot during that meal as they shared their stories of what it was like to run a shop in a Palestinian town while surrounded by hostile Jews most days. To be fair, we also heard from Jews what it was like to live in fear of attacks by Hamas and other radical Muslims—it's an insoluble situation in a tiny country. Still, that meal was one of the brightest spots in our week or so in Israel. I left with the feeling that, as Elise Boulding says above, that 'any meal, shared with love, can be an agape.'

- Have you ever experienced a "Eucharistic Feast" that wasn't during a church service? If so, what made it special to you?

Wednesday – The Walk to Emmaus

"Now on that same day two of them were going to a village called Emmaus, about seven miles from Jerusalem, and talking with each other about all these things that had happened. While they were talking and discussing, Jesus himself came near and went with them, but their eyes were kept from recognizing him. And he said to them, 'What are you discussing with each other while you walk along?' They stood still, looking sad. Then one of them, whose name was Cleopas, answered him, 'Are you the only stranger in Jerusalem who does not know the things that have taken place there in these days?' He asked them, 'What things?'

Encountering the risen Jesus

They replied, 'The things about Jesus of Nazareth, who was a prophet mighty in deed and word before God and all the people, and how our chief priests and leaders handed him over to be condemned to death and crucified him. But we had hoped that he was the one to redeem Israel. Yes, and besides all this, it is now the third day since these things took place. Moreover, some women in our group astounded us. They were at the tomb early this morning, and when they did not find his body there, they came back and told us that they had indeed seen a vision of angels who said that he was alive. Some of those who were with us went to the tomb and found it just as the women had said; but they did not see him.' Then he said to them, 'Oh, how foolish you are, and how slow of heart to believe all that the prophets have declared! Was it not necessary that the Messiah should suffer these things and then enter into his glory?' Then beginning with Moses and all the prophets, he interpreted to them the things about himself in all the scriptures." (Luke 24:13-27)

Jesus had already appeared to the women in the garden before this encounter on the road out of town. We know this because the full passage in Luke's Gospel includes their reporting to Jesus how the tomb was discovered empty. As a shepherd brings the strays back to the flock, Jesus goes after these two lost sheep leaving Jerusalem in disappointment and confusion.

The two disciples do not recognize Jesus. While this lack of recognition is common in resurrection appearances, it is odd that Jesus pretends not to know them or to have any idea about what has transpired this passover either. Jesus asks what has been going on in Jerusalem. Cleopas and the other disciple tell Jesus about how the one they thought was the Messiah had been put to death and then add, "Some women of our group astounded us. They were at the tomb early this morning, and when they did not find his body there, they came back and told us that they had indeed seen a vision of angels who said that he was alive. Some of those who were with us went to the tomb and found it just as the women had said; but they did not see him."

Jesus then lets the mask slip a little here and chides the disciples saying, "Oh, how foolish you are, and how slow of heart to believe all that the prophets have declared! Was it not necessary that the Messiah should suffer these things and then enter into his glory?"

Jesus then begins what must have been the best Bible study ever undertaken. Jesus patiently explains how everything he has done was predicted by the prophets. The ministry of Jesus in what we now call the New Testament dovetails perfectly into the Old Testament. Jesus paints a perfect picture of who the Messiah is. This is an important example of how, for some lessons, the time has to be right. Jesus had been predicting his death and resurrection, but his disciples failed to understand what he is saying. Only after his death and resurrection, can they see the words of the prophets in a new light. With the students ready to truly hear the lesson, the teacher appears on the Road to Emmaus to shed new light on those familiar passages, like the Suffering Servant in Isaiah, that no one had seen as messianic.

Encountering the risen Jesus

The two disciples still don't understand that they are walking with Jesus. Their eyes will be opened when the encounter continues in our reading this Saturday, but for now we see how the early church looked at the Old Testament anew with the hindsight provided by Jesus' life and ministry, his death and resurrection. Jesus himself interpreted the Hebrew scripture for them, giving them eyes to see what they had missed.

- Is there a story from scripture you have come to see differently based on your life experiences?

Thursday - Quotation

"Even of itself the teaching of the Blessed Paul is sufficient to give you a full assurance concerning those Divine Mysteries, of which having been deemed worthy, you have become of the same body and blood with Christ. For you have just heard him say distinctly, That our Lord Jesus Christ in the night in which He was betrayed, took bread, and when He had given thanks He broke it, and gave to His disciples, saying, Take, eat, this is My Body: and having taken the cup and given thanks, He said, Take, drink, this is My Blood. Since then He Himself declared and said of the Bread, This is My Body, who shall dare to doubt any longer? And since He has Himself affirmed and said, This is My Blood, who shall ever hesitate, saying, that it is not His blood?

"Consider therefore the Bread and the Wine not as bare

elements, for they are, according to the Lord's declaration, the Body and Blood of Christ; for even though sense suggests this to you, yet let faith establish you. Judge not the matter from the taste, but from faith be fully assured without misgiving, that the Body and Blood of Christ have been vouchsafed to you." (Lecture 22: *On the Body and Blood of Christ*)

"The Priest cries aloud, Lift up your hearts. For truly ought we in that most awful hour to have our heart on high with God, and not below, thinking of earth and earthly things. In effect therefore the Priest bids all in that hour to dismiss all cares of this life, or household anxieties, and to have their heart in heaven with the merciful God. Then ye answer, We lift them up unto the Lord: assenting to it, by your avowal. But let no one come here, who could say with his mouth, We lift up our hearts unto the Lord, but in his thoughts have his mind concerned with the cares of this life. At all times, rather, God should be in our memory but if this is impossible by reason of human infirmity, in that hour above all this should be our earnest endeavour." (Cyrils of Jerusalem's Lecture 23: *On the Sacred Liturgy and Communion*)

We go back to the Church of the Resurrection for quotations from Cyril of Jerusalem's final two lectures for those baptized at Easter who had received communion for the first time in the Easter Vigil. This meant that teaching about the mystery of what is happening in the Eucharist was an important part of what he wanted to share in his reflections in Easter Week.

In the penultimate talk, Cyril explains that the bread and wine will, of course, still taste as they always do, for they remain bread and wine even as they are now Christ's Body and Blood. Cyril is writing centuries before the Reformation, when precisely how one defined what happens in the Eucharist became something for which Christians were willing to be martyred. The Roman Catholic formula of Transubstantiation is defined in their catechism as, "the change of the whole substance of bread into the substance of the Body of Christ and of the whole substance of wine into the substance of the Blood of Christ." Using categories from Aristotle where the substance is the essence of a thing and the accidents are the outer form, this teaches that the outer form remains that of bread and wine while the essential nature of that bread truly becomes the body of Christ and the wine becomes the blood of Christ.

Anglicans, and therefore Episcopalians, adopted the formula of "real presence" to describe what happens to the elements in the Eucharistic Feast. Thomas Cranmer was the Archbishop of Canterbury who drafted the first Books of Common Prayer, one in 1549 that was an English rendering close to the Latin Mass of the time and the second in 1552, a text that reflected more of a reformed understanding of the Eucharist. In his reformed revision the sense is of a very real spiritual presence that he described as, "figuratively he is in the bread and wine, and spiritually he is in them that worthily eat and drink the bread and wine, but really, carnally, and corporally he is only in heaven." For the Archbishop who would be burned at the stake for his teachings, the sacraments were as Augustine of Hippo called them "visible words" that Cranmer saw as existing to spiritually nourish believers. He clearly taught that the Eucharist is not a mere memorial of the Last Supper Jesus shared with his disciples as Cranmer wrote, "As the bread is outwardly eaten indeed in the Lord's Supper, so is the very body of Christ inwardly by faith eaten of all them that come thereto in such sort as they ought to do, which eating nourisheth them into everlasting life."

Cyril moves in his last lecture to the disposition of the hearts of the worshippers, which we see also mattered to Archbishop Cranmer. In gathering for teaching in Easter Week, Cyril wanted to encourage the freshly initiated faithful to set aside the cares and anxieties of life so that worship becomes a time of having "their heart in heaven." But knowing this might not always be achieved, we should at least endeavor to do so. Knowing that Christ will be truly present with us in our worship, we prepare our hearts for union with God as we enter into worship. For both Cyril of Jerusalem and Thomas Cranmer know that it is quite possible to be so distracted that we miss what God is doing.

In our experience as worshippers, we (Victoria and Frank) know that whether our minds are stilled and focused on God or not, Jesus will still be with us. The Holy Trinity is much more reliable than our feelings. Yet it matters for us to approach worship open to receiving the presence of Christ in the spirit of this collect "Before Worship" on page 833 of the Book of Common Prayer:

> Almighty God, who pours out on all who desire it, the spirit of grace and of supplication; Deliver us, when we draw near to you, from coldness of heart and wanderings of mind, that with steadfast thoughts and kindled affections, we may worship you in spirit and in truth; through Jesus Christ our Lord. Amen.

- If a friend from another denomination asked what exactly we Episcopalians think about Communion, how would you answer them?

Friday – Frank's Reflection

Hospitality can turn any meal into a feast. It is all in how the meal is offered. I grew up in the south and so I know how to be polite, perhaps to a fault. I thought I knew hospitality. But I had a lot more to learn when I arrived in Tanzania for an internship during seminary.

Victoria and I had an experience of living in the Two-Thirds World when we spent two months in the Himalayan Kingdom of Nepal for two months on our honeymoon as we took pictures and interviewed people to write about the experience for magazines once home. It took a bit of a toll on our bodies as each of us got pretty sick at one point during that trip and in the process, we came home quite thin. So, I didn't mind that I left the United States a bit heavier than I would like after spending a year with all-you-can-eat buffets daily for lunch at the seminary. No problem, I thought as I imagined that I would lose weight during the internship anyway in the Anglican Church of Tanzania. But that is not what happened.

For one, I never got sick, but the main difference between the two trips was in being considered an honored guest. In Nepal, Victoria and I were tourists, staying in a motel and eating in restaurants. In Tanzania, I was always the guest, relying on the hospitality of others. The Canon whose congregation of St. Hilary's where I served, the Rev. Naftali Bikaka, told me that the family who invited me did not always eat like the meals I enjoyed. It was a special meal as they had a guest. This was quite humbling when you realize eating chicken did not mean running to the store. I was serving in Kibondo, a lovely town that is quite isolated on the far west side of the country, up against the Burundi border when many were refugeeing into Tanzania from their neighboring country. Connected to the world by deeply rutted red clay roads that become impassable in the rainy season, the chickens for most people in the area are those you raise from eggs. Deciding this is the day for this chicken means it isn't available for another meal later. It felt like I was the prodigal son feasting on fatted calves every time I was invited to a home for a meal. It was humbling to experience the radical hospitality of hosts sacrificing to offer a special meal. There were many such feasts that I well recall 27 years later.

Encountering the risen Jesus

Kids in the Bikaka Family that Frank lived with in Kibondo, Tanzania wait around the cook fire for breakfast to cook.

Every meal, breakfast, lunch, and dinner, included the East African staple, Ugali. This is a maize dish, like a thick polenta, that is picked up with your hands. I learned to roll some of the paste in my hand to form a ball, and make an indentation in it with my thumb, to create an edible spoon for sauce or beans, greens, and chicken. If that sounds messy, it is much less so than you would imagine as ugali made well doesn't stick to your fingers. And we would wash our hands before and after each meal.

I found out soon enough that the guest had to have seconds. This was not an option. Canon Bikaka taught me to get less on the first pass, so that I could get seconds, or even thirds as I also made sure everyone had eaten enough before doing so. Then I could eat the amount I wanted and my hosts would feel better about it. Honestly, it worked well anyway to get a little of everything and go back for what I wanted more of so it was not some weird guest chore to performatively seek out seconds. I also learned the word to show that the hospitality had been just right. After having seconds, and when being pressed to take more, I would say in Swahili, "inatosha" which means, "it is sufficient." The hosts would be pleased as their guest had been given enough.

I also remember fondly some tea and cookies that, while not a feast, were nonetheless an equally gracious gift. I had been watching World Cup soccer live in the street in Kibondo. It was set up by the Lembo twins, entrepreneuring Anglican brothers who charged people to watch a satellite fed large TV run on a generator. A young couple from St. Hilary's invited me back to their traditionally built "Swahili Home" with wood frame coated with mud for the walls and palm leaf roof over a packed earth floor. They noted the contrast between their home and some houses in the advertisements we saw during the breaks in the soccer match which included a couple having their morning coffee on the veranda beside their mansion overlooking the Mediterranean. I let them know that just as there are Tanzanians who also live in luxury beyond the reach of most everyone, that is true in Europe and America as well. What I couldn't adequately convey was how honored I was to be a guest in *their* home. The Chai and biscuits felt like a kind of communion in the sense of *koinonia*, something much more than shallow fellowship.

I heard in Tanzania that a guest brought blessings. I

thought that it meant, welcome a guest and blessings will come. I remember asking Canon Bikaka, "So, they want me to come visit so they can receive blessings?" "Yes," he replied, then he realized that I meant a sort of 'do this, get that' approach to hospitality. "No," he corrected. "The Guest is the blessing. They don't host you so that God will give them something in return. Having you come to visit is the gift." In every invitation, I also experienced the blessing of being the guest of people who understood more about hospitality than I had previously experienced, which turned every time we shared food into a feast.

- When have you been offered radical hospitality? What was it like to be the recipient of that gift?

Saturday – The Breaking of the Bread

"As they came near the village to which they were going, he walked ahead as if he were going on. But they urged him strongly, saying, 'Stay with us, because it is almost evening and the day is now nearly over.' So he went in to stay with them. When he was at the table with them, he took bread, blessed and broke it, and gave it to them. Then their eyes were opened, and they recognized him; and he vanished from their sight. They said to each other, 'Were not our hearts burning within us while he was talking to us on the road, while he was opening the scriptures to us?' That same hour they got up and returned to Jerusalem; and they found the eleven and their companions gathered together. They were saying, 'The Lord has risen indeed, and he has appeared to Simon!' Then they told what had happened on the road, and how he had been made known to them in the breaking of the bread." (Luke 24:28-35)

As we take up the story we began on Wednesday, Cleopas and the other disciple reach Emmaus. Jesus intends to keep going. The Greek word translated here "as if he were going on" means "pretending to go on." The disciples prove themselves to be Christ followers, offering the stranger hospitality. Then at the meal that evening, the stranger who is the guest becomes the host. Jesus takes the bread, blesses the bread, breaks the bread and gives the bread to those gathered for the meal. Then comes the "Eureka!" moment in breaking the bread.

How very Jesus. This is exactly what Jesus did when he fed the thousands on a hillside with two weensy fish and five barley loaves. In all these accounts of the feeding of thousands, Jesus takes the bread, blesses the bread, breaks the bread and gives the bread. More recently, Jesus did the same at The Last Supper, just a few nights earlier. On that night, Jesus took, blessed, broke and gave the bread. Jesus explained that he was the bread. Jesus, who had already been taken and blessed by God, was broken by man on Good Friday and now on Easter, this same Jesus was being given back to the world. Then they knew the stranger on the road was Jesus.

As soon as awareness dawns on them, Jesus is gone.

Encountering the risen Jesus

Vanished. But the two who had been slipping out of town alone had experienced the risen Jesus. At once they retraced their steps back to the upper room in Jerusalem. The seven mile slog out from town is now a quick trot back. Cleopas and the unnamed disciple learned that Peter too had seen the risen Jesus. Then they added their own experience on the Road to Emmaus to the stories of the resurrected Lord, telling what had happened on the road and how he was made known to them in the breaking of the bread.

The pattern of the encounter on the Road to Emmaus is the same pattern for our Sunday worship as we first hear the Word of God read and commented on and then we move to the sacrament of the Eucharist. Scripture and Bread. Word and Sacrament. We gather to hear the word of God in our scripture readings, in the songs we sing (which are scriptural as well) and through the words of the sermon, we spend time in the word. Next, we will move to the table and on behalf of our risen Lord, The Celebrant will take, bless, break and give the bread—the bread that is Christ's presence among us. Like Cleopas and the unnamed disciple, we have found that when we gather for word and sacrament, we can depend on Jesus showing up. Like all of the resurrection appearances, the Road to Emmaus matters not just because Jesus was once made known to two disillusioned disciples, but as we find that Jesus is still made known in word and sacrament.

- When has an experience led you to certainty that God had shown up?

Holy Mysteries
SUNDAY – FEAST REVISITED

The Feasts of Passover and the Eucharist don't just look back, but they also direct us toward the future. The Passover does look back to the Exodus but it also points forward to the coming of the Messiah. While the Eucharist looks back to Jesus, who we know to be the Messiah, it looks forward to his return in glory.

The Passover can help us to better understand the Eucharist. During the Jewish Passover celebration, a glass of wine is set out for the Prophet Elijah. It is hoped that Elijah will come join the celebration. Setting out a glass of wine for Elijah reminds those at the table that another kind of deliverance is yet to come. As they are called to look back and remember the Exodus, they are called to look forward and anticipate the Messiah. The prophet Malachi wrote that Elijah would return before the Messiah comes, so at each Passover meal, a glass of wine is at the ready to welcome Elijah on his return.

In seminary, we took part in a traditional Passover celebration with our daughter, Griffin, in the home of a Jewish family. This was arranged by Rabbi Jack Moline, who was teaching the Introduction to Judaism course I was taking at the time. This was the first time we had attended a Passover seder. At the end of the meal, a child is sent to the door to look for the prophet Elijah. Elijah is expected to return before the Messiah.

When the time came, Griffin, who was seven at the time, was the only school-aged child at the seder. She was told about

Elijah and how he was expected to return. Then Griffin was asked to go to the door to check for Elijah. Griffin was scared and asked me to go along with her. Fearfully she opened the front door. She looked out tentatively at first, and then cautiously stuck her head further out the door. Finally she stepped outside and carefully looked the street up and down. Elijah was not in sight. We returned to the Passover table and let everyone know that Elijah had not come.

That night, as we were putting her to bed, Griffin asked, "Why do they want a child to go to the door to look for Elijah?" I hadn't thought of it before, but when she asked the question, the answer was clear. I asked Griffin, "When we went to look for Elijah, did you think he might really be there this time?" Griffin said she did. I told her, "That's why they send a child. Because, a child will look hard, and believe that Elijah will really come this time."

Jews all around the world celebrate the Passover in anticipation of the Messiah as well as in remembrance of the Exodus. Children go to the door and look for Elijah. Each child wonders if he or she would be the one to see him first.

Have we lost that sense of wonder? Each time we celebrate the Eucharist, we say that it is to celebrate the memorial of our redemption until our Lord returns. Jesus didn't tell his disciples that the Passover on the night before he died was his last meal with them ever. He said he wouldn't partake of the bread and wine until they did so together in his father's heavenly kingdom. The Eucharist is not The Last Supper for us if we can recapture the air of anticipation. Each time we celebrate the Eucharist it is to be the next-to-the-last-supper.

Holy Mysteries

What if we viewed the Eucharist as The Next to the Last Supper instead? Not a meal, but an appetizer. The main course will come at the heavenly banquet. The Last Supper doesn't come at the end of the story, because the end of the story has not yet occurred. The Eucharist also points forward to his coming again. That will be a Last Supper to remember. In the meantime, we wait, we watch, and we take part in the meal before the last. The foretaste of heavenly glory here on earth.

- Are there any memories from your childhood of taking part in a liturgy or other ritual that stand out to you? How do you see that same liturgy or ritual differently now?

Rembrandt van Rjin's study of The Last Supper after Leonardo da Vinci (1634-35)

Week IV
Oil

Monday – Introducing Oil

"And he [Jacob] was afraid and said,
'How awesome is this place!
This is none other than the house of God,
and this is the gate of heaven.'
So Jacob rose early in the morning,
and he took the stone that he had put under his head
and set it up for a pillar and poured oil on the top of it.
He called that place Bethel."

-Genesis 28:17-19a

In his lectures offered in Easter Week, Cyril connected the water of baptism closely with holy oil as he referred to "Holy Baptism and the Mystical Chrism" together. The chrism is olive oil scented with additional essential oils, especially balsam, and blessed by a bishop for use in the sacrament. This special oil is one of the many ways that oil has been entwined with religion in many cultures through all recorded history. And while it was often used for anointing and still is, olive oil was linked to one's very life in the Ancient Near East. Not only was it used for oil in lamps, but also to moisturize in a desert environment and to clean the hair and the body as well as in healing.

Oil is mentioned 213 times in the Old and New Testaments and the Apocrypha. Certainly, this included many references to anointing someone with oil as a king was anointed for service and the Messiah is "the Annointed One."

The religious aspect of oil is prominent as being very much a part of our sacramental rites from baptism through death. Oil can be used in baptism, confirmation, and is used in healing prayers. In the Book of Common Prayer, after a person is baptized, we read:

> "Then the Bishop or Priest places a hand on the person's head, marking on the forehead the sign of the cross [using Chrism if desired] and saying to each one, "N., you are sealed by the Holy Spirit in Baptism and marked as Christ's own for ever. Amen."

Powerful words. Marked as Christ's own for ever. Until the end of time. Forever. Eternally.

Olive oil was woven into the lives of the people of the Mediterranean and was connected to health and healing and so only natural for it to be used by God in bringing both physical and spiritual health and healing. Our temporal natural lives and the life eternal are connected of course and God is always making the common into something holy.

Encountering the risen Jesus

In the parable we know as The Good Samaritan, Jesus refers to oil used in healing (Luke 10:33-35), "A Samaritan while traveling came upon him, and when he saw him, he was moved with compassion. He went to him and bandaged his wounds, *treating them with oil and wine.* [italics mine] Then he put him on his own animal, brought him to an inn, and took care of him. The next day he took out two denarii, gave them to the innkeeper, and said, 'Take care of him, and when I come back, I will repay you whatever more you spend.'"

Anointing of the Sick is the sacramental rite called unction, naming it for the oil used in the rite. Even churches that don't maintain its use in baptism, commonly anoint with olive oil as a part of healing prayers. In an Episcopal Church, when the person is to be anointed, "the Priest dips a thumb in the holy oil [oil that has previously been blessed], and makes the sign of the cross on the sick person's forehead, saying, "N., I anoint you with oil in the Name of the Father, and of the son, and of the Holy Spirit. Amen."

In the Catechism in the back of our Prayer Book, we read of the sacraments and then the question is asked "Is God's activity limited to these rites?" The answer being, "God does not limit himself to these rites; they are patterns of countless ways by which God uses material things to reach out to us."

The Holy Trinity, whom the cosmos can not contain, uses matter, like olive oil, in conveying the power and presence of the living God within space and time. We know through the revelation of scripture that God is both in all things and beyond all things. The "God with us" proclaimed in calling Jesus "Emmanuel," shows the immanence of God, God is in all things. But unlike in pantheism, where God is identified with the universe, which is a manifestation of the divine, we know that the creator is not contained within the creation. Augustine of Hippo wrote that the divine is both within me and beyond me saying that God, "more inward than my most inward part, higher than the highest element within me."

God is in everything, but also beyond all matter, and is not bound by space and time. This transcendence of God is captured in scripture that, for example, describes God's holiness. We also see this aspect of the divine in texts that make it clear that the inner life of the Holy Trinity is beyond our power to comprehend, "For my thoughts are not your thoughts, nor are your ways my ways. For as the heavens are higher than the earth, so are my ways higher than your ways, my thoughts higher than your thoughts." – Isaiah 55:8.

The God beyond our comprehension comes to us in ways we can experience in the natural world. In using the natural world, using the stuff of life like oil, to reveal the divine to us, the transcendent God is with us in our lives that are bound by space and time.

- Have you had a priest offer healing prayers for you? If so, what was that experience like for you?
- Do you tend to conceive of God more as with us in a very personal way or beyond us in being entirely other?

Encountering the risen Jesus
Tuesday – Victoria's Reflection

> "Sacrifice and asceticism are usually indicators of False Self religion.... Ascetic practices have far too much social and ego payoff, which is why Jesus advised against anything pious or generous being done publicly (Matthew 6:1-4, 16-18): 'Don't even let your left hand know what your right hand is doing,' he says. External religion is also dangerous."
>
> -Richard Rohr

To be completely honest, I did not become truly interested in the Sacraments until I was in my early 40s and in the process of becoming a Tertiary in the Third Order, Society of Saint Francis. It's not that they weren't important to me—I found meaning in partaking of the Eucharist as well as in Marriage and Baptism and Confirmation—but they just were, just a part of life as an Episcopalian. And because of my husband's call, I was aware of Holy Orders and Unction.

And, as I continued through the process, I learned more about reconciliation of a penitent as confession is required annually in the Order. But what really stuck with me was what was stated in the Principles of Order on Day Fifteen:

> "The First Way of Service, cont'd—The heart of our prayer is the Eucharist, in which we share with other Christians the renewal of our union with our Lord and Savior in his sacrifice, remembering his death and receiving his spiritual food."

Holy Mysteries

So, as I was encouraged to do, my Rule of Life included receiving the Eucharist at least two times a week. At first this was really easy to accomplish as we were at King of Peace in Kingsland at the time and I attended all the services—Wednesday, Sunday, and Holy Days at first, and later, two to three weekend services instead of just one.

Later, when we moved to Savannah when Frank became Canon to the Ordinary to Bishop Benhase, I attended the weekly service at the Diocesan Chapel, including the new chapel when the Diocesan Office moved to East 34th Street.

This continued after Frank was elected Bishop in 2019 and we moved into 2020 planning his Consecration in May. And then, as we will never forget—COVID. Plans for the Consecration rapidly devolved until we were down to 11 people and a film crew at Christ Church. The Presiding Bishop wasn't able to make it because of travel/pandemic reasons and we scrambled to get two more of the three required Bishops. Presiding Bishop Michael Curry named Bishop Scott Benhase as the chief consecrator in his stead. Bishop Rob Wright of Atlanta and our current Presiding Bishop Sean Rowe was the third.

By May 30, weekly Eucharists were a thing of the past with filmed Morning Prayer (and sometimes Evening) being the standard. When we did film a Eucharist for the online service, it was knowing that those watching could not take part, which left me feeling guilty knowing that so many people were longing for Communion in both senses of the word. What a change! I had gone from being a Eucharist junkie, in a manner of speaking, to realizing that I could get

Encountering the risen Jesus

as much meaning from a virtually shared Morning Prayer each Sunday as Christ is present in each.

By the time we started back to relatively normal worship and in-person Visitations in 2021, I was in a completely different place—finding meaning in our communal worship and sharing of the Eucharist rather than it being all about myself and partaking of Communion.

As Franciscan Saint Bonaventure said:

The Rev. Kyle Mackey communes Victoria at St. Patrick's in Albany.

> "[God] is an intelligible space whose center is everywhere and whose circumference is nowhere. ... [God] is within all things, but not enclosed, outside all things but not excluded, above all things but not aloof, below all things but not debased. ... [God] is supremely one and all-inclusive, [God] is therefore 'all in all'."

Yes, I can commune with God alone and in silence, but without worshiping in Community, you cannot find completeness. Even hermits and anchorites over the years had contact with people—sometimes by attending services, sometimes by serving as spiritual counselors, and in other ways—but even in devoting most of their time to God in silence and prayer they still needed community.

- How important is it to you to take part in a weekly Eucharist?
- What aspects of a weekly service of Communion are most important to you?

Wednesday – The Breath

"When it was evening on that day, the first day of the week, and the doors of the house where the disciples had met were locked for fear of the Jews, Jesus came and stood among them and said, 'Peace be with you.' After he said this, he showed them his hands and his side. Then the disciples rejoiced when they saw the Lord. Jesus said to them again, 'Peace be with you. As the Father has sent me, so I send you.' When he had said this, he breathed on them and said to them, 'Receive the Holy Spirit. If you forgive the sins of any, they are forgiven them; if you retain the sins of any, they are retained.'" (John 20:19-23)

The disciples are afraid that they will be found. Trapped by fear, they wait in confusion not knowing what to do next. Then Jesus appears in their midst, standing among them in the flesh. John tells us that "the disciples rejoiced when they saw the Lord." I suspect that this is a case where words fail to capture the meaning, the excitement that is

Encountering the risen Jesus

beyond words. I mean they "rejoiced when they saw the Lord." Rejoiced is putting it mildly. Jesus was so brutally killed on Friday and now he is alive again. To be in the middle of unbearable grief and then have the Lord returned to them must have created indescribable joy. Jesus was back. Jesus was home. They were all together again. Everything would be back to normal.

But, of course, that wasn't God's plan. It wasn't time for the same old, same old. It was time for the next phase of the plan. It was time to move ahead into a new ministry. Jesus had shown the disciples the way. Now it was their turn. Jesus said, "As the Father has sent me, so I send you." Then he breathed on them. It was the life-giving breath of God. It was the same breath that blew over the waters at creation. The same breath that God blew into Adam and brought him to life. That same life-giving breath flowed over and in the disciples. It was the Spirit of God. Jesus called on them to receive the Spirit. It was to equip them for the work ahead. Jesus was leaving, but the Spirit was remaining.

What Jesus accomplishes here is to set them free from fear and to inspire them. Jesus greets them saying "Peace be with you;" he breathes on them. This is inspirational in its literal sense. To inspire is to put breath into something. Breathing into his disciples rings in the ears of those immersed in the Biblical story as familiar. For God breathed life into Adam in the same way. This is intentional. What is taking place is new life, new creation. Just as God breathed life into the first man, so too Jesus, the second person of the Trinity, breathes new life into humanity.

Holy Mysteries

The apostle Paul will make this clear when he later writes, "If anyone is in Christ: New Creation." The breath that Jesus gives is specifically named as the third person of the Trinity—the Holy Spirit. It is the Holy Spirit working in and through us that animates the new life. It is the Holy Spirit that breathes the potential for resurrection into our dying bodies.

What is taking place in John's Gospel is that Jesus appears soon after his resurrection to commission the first Christians to go out with the Good News and in doing so he inspired them with the gift of the Holy Spirit to give them new life within them. Then he called on them to forgive or retain sins. That was their commission. That was what those with a new life were to do.

But as we see in our look at scripture, forgiving sins has nothing to do with a pronouncement, "You are forgiven," and everything to do with helping someone come to faith. We are to assist others in seeing Jesus rightly. By the power and inspiration of the Holy Spirit, we are to help others to come to know that Jesus is God's son and that through him we can have a new life. This is why early Christian writers would write of baptism. For those early Christian authors, anyone who understood rightly who Jesus is and believed in him would naturally seek out baptism, that opportunity for a public profession of faith. The way you could be part of forgiving sins is helping someone come to know Jesus. The way you retain sins is by holding still, keeping quiet, and not speaking up when the Holy Spirit gives you an opportunity.

Sins are forgiven or retained when one decides whether

Encountering the risen Jesus

to come to faith in Jesus in response to hearing the Gospel. Any Christian is, therefore, not to be the judge of another as to whether they are right and wrong. We are instead to be witnesses to what we have experienced in Jesus.

That's it. We either share God's love or not. If we share God's love, others may find the path to forgiveness. If we withhold God's love we are working to retain that person's sins. Jesus offered the first followers new life, new creation, trusting them to offer that new life to others. Jesus has given you new life and he expects you to share that gift as well. It was for this that you, like those first followers, have been inspired.

- Do you feel that your church offers that witness, or signs of new life that only come from God, in such a way that people long for a relationship with God?
- Are there ways that you do this in your own life?

Thursday - Quotation

"Having been baptized into Christ, and put on Christ, ye have been made conformable to the Son of God; for God having foreordained us unto adoption as sons, made us to be conformed to the body of Christ's glory. Having therefore become partakers of Christ, ye are properly called Christs, and of you God said, Touch not My Christs, or anointed. Now ye have been made Christs, by receiving the antitype of the Holy Ghost; and all things have been wrought in you by imitation, because ye are images of Christ....

"For as Christ after His Baptism, and the visitation of the Holy Ghost, went forth and vanquished the adversary, so likewise ye, after Holy Baptism and the Mystical Chrism, having put on the whole armour of the Holy Ghost, are to stand against the power of the adversary, and vanquish it, saying, 'I can do all things through Christ which strengtheneth me.'

"Having been counted worthy of this Holy Chrism, ye are called Christians, verifying the name also by your new birth. For before you were deemed worthy of this grace, you had properly no right to this title, but were advancing on your way towards being Christians.

"Moreover, you should know that in the old Scripture there lies the symbol of this Chrism. For what time Moses imparted to his brother the command of God, and made him High-priest, after bathing in water, he anointed him; and Aaron was called Christ or Anointed, evidently from the typical Chrism. So also the High-priest, in advancing Solomon to the kingdom, anointed him after he had bathed in Gihon. To them however these things happened in a figure, but to you not in a figure, but in truth; because ye were truly anointed by the Holy Ghost." (Cyril of Jerusalem's Lecture 21: *On Chrism*)

In his lecture on the holy oil of chrism, blessed by the bishop for use in baptisms, Cyril of Jerusalem described how anointing with chrism is an antitype–something we find in the New Testament that is foreshadowed by a symbol or type in the Old Testament. In the Old Testament, one would be anointed for roles including those of priest (Aaron in Leviticus 8:12), prophet (Elisha in I Kings 19:16), and king (Saul and David in I Samuel 10:1,16:13 and Solomon in I Kings 1:38 as Cyril notes above). These persons anointed for important roles pointed toward The Anointed One, the Messiah. As baptized Christians, marked with the sign of the cross in baptism, Cyril says we are rightly called "Christs" and "Christian."

The word "Christ" in Greek is foreshadowed by "Messiah" in Hebrew. Both refer to anointed ones. He makes the case that as we are anointed by oil in our baptisms, we are anointed ones and therefore worthy to be called Christian, which means "A little Christ." Cyril says, "You properly had no right to this title" as we did not earn or deserve this grace. But we are called to live more and more into being Christ-like. Our faith in Jesus is not meant to be static, but ever dynamic, always stretching us as we seek to grow more and more into the image and likeness of God. Each of us who have been justified before God through our faith in Jesus are called to the ongoing work of sanctification. Sanctification is the process of becoming more and more Christ-like over a lifetime and beyond. We won't ever get this perfect, but we can grow in grace over time to more fully be what we already are, Christian.

In the 1979 Book of Common Prayer, the newly baptized, still dripping wet, is marked with the sign of the cross by the bishop or priest who typically uses the oil of chrism for this action as they say, "*N.*, you are sealed by the Holy Spirit in

Baptism and marked as Christ's own for ever."

- Has there been a baptism you witnessed where these words had particular resonance?

Friday – Frank's Reflection

Chrism oil is closely connected with the role of a bishop and as I look back on nearly five years as the chief pastor, what comes to mind most are the times when chrism has mingled with tears of joy. By October of 2020, I had been bishop for 130 days, yet had not made any official parish visitations as we were in that early phase of the COVID-19 pandemic. Victoria and I had been traveling to towns across the Diocese to record worship that we offered online each week. We had created seventeen of these before I was able to gather in person with the clergy of the Diocese for three in-person liturgies.

On October 7, we were outdoors at the Flowing Wells Campus owned by Good Shepherd in Augusta. Canon Loren Lasch preached a beautiful sermon of how the Holy Spirit shows up in the most surprising of ways in worship unlike any we imagined by using the story of having communion with saltines and water with a man who was dying and that was all he could receive. I blessed oil for chrism for the first time under those unusual circumstances, so grateful to be with diocesan clergy. We repeated this again on the lawn at St. Anne's in Tifton on October 22, and then at Honey

Creek on the 29th. One priest from Savannah later said that the fairly brief Eucharist took 3 hours of driving to get there and home and it was completely worth it. I found them so nourishing as we were able to be together in person. The chrism I blessed was used right away as baptisms continued even when large, in-person worship in the church was not yet possible.

Chrism is used in baptisms, and may also be used in confirmation, and the tradition of the church and our Prayer Book and Book of Occasional Services reserve this oil as to be exclusively blessed by a bishop. This blessing can happen in a baptism or confirmation liturgy where the bishop is present, but usually occurs in an annual Chrism Mass in Holy Week. This connects me as chief pastor to all of the baptisms in the Diocese when the oil is used to mark the newly baptized with the sign of the cross.

A confirmation I did in a home was another occasion when tears and chrism were part of the same liturgy. In June of 2021, I pulled up to the curb of Kathy's home in a gated community. I knew a number of Episcopalians lived on the same street and was surprised that I had to walk some distance to the house for the cars lining the road. Kathy was a home-bound parishioner in Hospice care who wanted to reaffirm her faith and have me lay on hands and pray for her, confirming the promises made in baptism on her behalf many years earlier. Twenty friends were gathered in her living and dining rooms with the hardback Books of Common Prayer from the church balanced on their knees. It was a touching liturgy as was evident that Kathy was far

Holy Mysteries

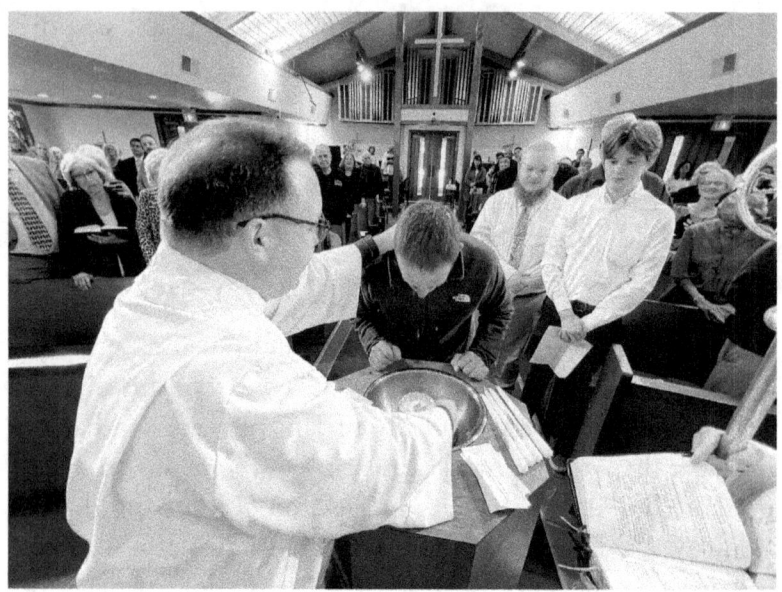

The Very Rev. Al Crumpton baptizes his brother Brad at Our Savior in Martinez.

from alone in crying as I marked the sign of the cross on her forehead with the oil. The worship was as beautiful in its own way as any cathedral service for those of us joining with her in the confirmation and Eucharist in her home.

A last link between chrism and tears of joy were the four adult baptisms at Our Savior in Martinez in November 2022. I watched as the Very Rev. Al Crumpton baptized his brother, Brad, and sister-in-law Dori, and I got to confirm them. Both Al and Brad were sure this was something that would never happen, but grace has a way of finding a path into someone's heart when it seems there is no way. There was a lot of joy to go around that Sunday.

Encountering the risen Jesus

These few examples are just a taste of the joy of this call that is so closely connected to the balsam-scented olive oil that I get to bless as a bishop.

- When have you experienced or seen others with tears of joy in a liturgy?

Saturday – The Touch

"But Thomas (who was called the Twin), one of the twelve, was not with them when Jesus came. So the other disciples told him, 'We have seen the Lord.' But he said to them, 'Unless I see the mark of the nails in his hands, and put my finger in the mark of the nails and my hand in his side, I will not believe.' A week later his disciples were again in the house, and Thomas was with them. Although the doors were shut, Jesus came and stood among them and said, 'Peace be with you.' Then he said to Thomas, 'Put your finger here and see my hands. Reach out your hand and put it in my side. Do not doubt but believe.' Thomas answered him, 'My Lord and my God!' Jesus said to him, 'Have you believed because you have seen me? Blessed are those who have not seen and yet have come to believe.'" (John 20:24-29)

While he is sometimes referred to as Doubting Thomas, this disciple was actually quite sure of one thing. Namely, unless he could see the marks of the nails in Jesus' hands and put his finger in the mark of Jesus' hands and in

Jesus' side, he could never believe that his friend and teacher Jesus had been raised from the dead. Thomas was crystal clear about what he needed. For a week straight, Thomas lived with that doubt. Thomas was surrounded by the disciples who hadn't been out on an errand the previous week. Unlike Thomas, they each seen the risen Jesus heard him speak the words, "Peace be with you."

Jesus had appeared to the rest on Sunday evening, the same Sunday of the resurrection. All through the week, the disciples would have tried to persuade Thomas. Yes, he had really suffered and really died, but God had raised Jesus from the dead and he was back in the wounded flesh to prove it. Thomas did not waver in his demand, "Unless I see the mark of the nails in his hands, and put my finger in the mark of the nails and in his side, I will not believe."

The insistence on seeing the visual proof of the resurrection underlines the fact that Jesus is not a spirit or ghost but fully human. Christ being seen and known in the flesh after his resurrection is fundamental for John. So he tells us what happened next when Jesus came back and Thomas is with the group in the upper room. Jesus greets them with the traditional, "Peace be with you," he turns to Thomas to address him. "Put your finger here and see my hands," Jesus tells him. "Reach out your hand and put it in my side. Do not doubt but believe." Without a word to Thomas about his unfaithfulness, Jesus gives him exactly what he asks for. The doubting disciple has already seen Jesus, but Jesus also offers to allow Thomas to touch his hands and his side.

Thomas no longer needs that confirmation. Seeing and

hearing the risen Jesus, he passes from the state of doubt to the state of faith. He is now convinced that the man he sees is the same Jesus that he knew in life. Without hesitation, he responds: "My Lord and my God." Thomas becomes the first disciple to express his faith in Christ this way. Jesus is now his "Lord and God."

For Thomas, the change is radical. He goes from the skeptic unbeliever to delivering a declaration of faith that, though short, is the ultimate statement of Christology. This passage shows that doubts are not only acceptable, but to be encouraged as Jesus did not berate Thomas for unbelief, but gave him what he needed to recover his faith. Doubt is a sign of an active faith. Lay your doubts out there. Give all your doubts to God in prayer. Even if you doubt God can hear and answer prayer, pray about that. Consider what you believe and offer any remaining doubts and give it over to God.

The story continues with a question and a blessing as Thomas' exclamation is followed by Jesus, asking: "Have you believed because you have seen me?" Then he adds, "Blessed are those who have not seen and yet have come to believe."

This beatitude proposes a different kind of faith, a faith that does not depend on seeing for believing. Who are 'the Blessed' in this case? Certainly, the Christians that John wrote his Gospel for were, for the most part, born after the resurrection and the ascension of Christ. Jesus proclaims them blessed because they arrived at the state of believing in the risen Lord without the proof of having seen. Coming to faith after seeing the risen Christ was limited to the disciples

Holy Mysteries

and those who Jesus chose to show himself to (think Paul on the road to Damascus, for example). John was aware of this and therefore introduces the way of believing without seeing by coming to believe based on the testimony of the apostolic eyewitnesses.

God revealed God's own self to us through Jesus the Christ and continues to do so. God remains at work in our lives through the power of the Holy Spirit. God wants to be present in your life no matter what doubts you have, but naming those doubts and seeking answers is helpful. We (Victoria and Frank) have found that when we are honest about our doubts, that God shows up in ways that strengthen our faith. We have experiences of the Spirit showing up in ways that defy any other explanation. When we, in the words of scripture, "taste and see" we do experience that God is good and faithful.

- Has there ever been a time when you felt you couldn't believe something without seeing it?
- How easy or difficult is it for you to have faith in a God you cannot see?

Encountering the risen Jesus
SUNDAY – OIL REVISITED

> "If you will only heed his every commandment
> that I am commanding you today—
> loving the Lord your God, and serving him
> with all your heart and with all your soul—
> then he will give the rain for your land in its season,
> the early rain and the later rain,
> and you will gather in your grain, your wine, and your oil."

-Deuteronomy 11:13-14

Oil was such an essential staple of life in the Ancient Near East, it was one of the blessings promised to those who follow Moses' Law. As we have seen this week, while most uses were common, olive oil was instrumental in anointing prophets, priests, and kings as well as its use in healing. These marked oil as a staple that God can and does bless and make holy. Making the common into the holy is so very like the Holy Trinity. This is what God does in Jesus in making the common people of God holy. We are called saints, meaning holy ones, not because we deserve that name, but because of God's love. We are not made just by our actions, but seen as justified because of Jesus' redemption.

But this action on God's part is not to set us apart from others any more than prophets were to separate themselves from the lost and hurting world they were anointed to call back to faithfulness to God. In his book *Being Christian: Baptism, Bible, Eucharist, Prayer*, Rowan Williams captures this well in writing about baptism:

> "To be able to say, 'I'm baptized' is not to claim an extra dignity, let alone a sort of privilege that keeps you separate from and superior to the rest of the human race, but to claim a new level of solidarity with other people. It is to accept that to be a Christian is to be affected—you might even say contaminated—by the mess of humanity. This is very paradoxical. Baptism is a ceremony in which we are washed, cleansed and re-created. It is also a ceremony in which we are pushed into the middle of a human situation that may hurt us, and that will not leave us untouched or unsullied. And the gathering of baptized people is therefore not a convocation of those who are privileged, elite and separate, but of those who have accepted what it means to be in the heart of a needy, contaminated, messy world. To put it another way, you don't go down into the waters of the Jordan without stirring up a great deal of mud!"

As that community that has been pushed into the messiness of life, we are a people blessed to have olive oil in the church (and often in the glove box of the priest's car) to use in offering healing prayers. This is a sign of the larger ways we are to offer healing, both in the church and well beyond. We are to not only feed those experiencing homelessness, but we are also to work to lessen the likelihood of someone living on the streets. In doing so, we demonstrate that we see the

Encountering the risen Jesus

dignity in every human being as someone made in the image and likeness of God.

That work of healing is not, of course, the work of a priest or deacon alone. This is where the old word "Parson," which meant a representative person, is helpful. A priest is to represent Christ in such a way as to encourage the whole congregation to do the same, visiting someone sick or in prison, as an example of what every member of the Body of Christ is to do.

We are not called away from the mess of life, but called back into it as people blessed with healing oil to offer the sick, and the oil of Chrism with which to mark others as Christ's own forever as they come out of the waters of baptism. We have something to offer to the chaos of the world, our experience of the living God, that we can use to point others to that same healing and wholeness we have found and that we need again and again.

- Have you experienced something ordinary, whether an object or experience, being much more than it first seemed?

Week V
Participation

Monday – Introducing Participation

> "I have seen the Totality,
> received not in essence, but by participation.
> When you light a flame from a flame,
> it is the same flame that you receive."
>
> -St. Symeon the New Theologian

We enter more fully this week into the mystery of the Holy Trinity. We could know nothing of the life of God if God had not revealed this to us, three persons, inseparable and yet each distinct. The doctrine of Trinity is far from esoteric, as it could first seem. We are called in the words of the Collect for the Second Sunday of Christmas to, "share the divine life of him who humbled himself to share our humanity, your Son Jesus Christ."

Through sharing in the love that is in the heart of God, we participate in the divine life. When we express the agape love we see in Jesus, that is more concerned for the other person than with oneself, we connect more deeply with the God who is love. The Episcopal priest and mystic Cynthia Bourgeault touches on this in writing, "To mourn is to touch directly the substance of divine compassion."

Before anything else existed, there was a communion of three separate persons of the Godhead who created everything, including you and me, out of love for love. The Trinity is not just one being but persons in relationships and communion, from before time and forever. This is why you were created, to be in healthy, loving, generative relationship with God and all creation. And out of this web of relationships comes both your salvation and the redemption of all creation.

The Holy Trinity is God's self-revelation that offers us insight into creation and redemption as God invites us into a dynamic and loving relationship in which we see and know that we are meant to be in communion with and participants in the divine life. This reveals how close all creation is meant to be, and how the world, broken as it is, offers the connections that matter more than what separates us.

The word Trinity never appears in the Bible. Yet, in passages like the Great Commission that Jesus gave to his disciples in Matthew's Gospel, we read of Jesus asking them to baptize new followers in the name of the Father and of the Son and of the Holy Spirit. And there is another Trinitarian formulation in Second Corinthians where Paul states: "The grace of the Lord Jesus Christ, the love of God, and the communion of the Holy Spirit be with all of you."

All through scripture there is both the idea of one God

and the description of the Father, Son, and Holy Spirit. The early church writer Tertullian coined the word, Trinity. He also created "Person" and "Substance" to describe what his mind saw when he contemplated the scriptures about the three-in-one God. Tertullian loved to create new Latin words. He created 509 nouns, 284 adjectives and 161 verbs. Not all of his created words were used by other writers, but many of his new words lived on, particularly Trinity, Person, and Substance.

Tertullian said that there is a Trinity—a threeness—with three separate persons of a single substance. The analogies we use to describe what we mean by 'Trinity' tend to fall short and the analogies pushed too far end up in heresy. Saint Patrick's three petals forming a single shamrock is one of the most common, though the Irish saint may not have used the illustration himself. There are other analogies for the Trinity, like H_2O, which is capable of being steam, water, and ice. Our words are helpful, but they fall short of the ability to describe God. Whatever language we use, we know God is not two dudes and a dove. Even so, the interconnectedness God tells us is within the divine self matches the interconnectedness of all things that mystics teach us and experience reveals at least partially.

John Wesley put it this way, "Bring me a worm that can comprehend a man, and then I will show you a man that can comprehend the triune God!" The Trinity is a mystery in that we see the truth of it, but there is more than we can fully understand. This is not unlike the love we see among humans or even among humans and pets. We know so much about those we love, and yet occasions arise in which it is revealed that there was more to discover in the relationship with our child or spouse, parents or friends. We can and do know of God from God, by the Revelation of scripture, from the way God is revealed in nature, and through that most perfect Revelation of God, Jesus the Christ. And yet, there is more than we know, a mystery that is deeper than our minds can fathom.

This Holy Mystery also shows how we are to be connected not just to God, but to other people. The Croatian theologian Miroslav Volf put it this way,

> "Faith leads human beings into the divine communion. One cannot, however, have a self-enclosed communion with the Triune God–a 'foursome,' as it were–for the Christian God is not a private deity. Communion with this God is at once also communion with those others who have entrusted themselves in faith to the same God. Hence one and the same act of faith places a person into a new relationship both with God and with all others who stand in communion with God."

We are meant to be sharers in the divine life. We were created out of the overflowing love of God to experience and share love with God and with one another. In this way, we participate in the divine nature, which is love and that love is to draw us not just closer to God, but also closer to other people.

- What way of explaining or describing the Holy Trinity has connected with you?

Tuesday – Victoria's Reflection

> "God is gathering us out of all regions
> till he can make resurrection of our own hearts
> from the very earth and teach us that
> we are all of one substance, and members of one another;
> for the one who loves his neighbor loves God,
> and the one who loves God, loves his own soul."
>
> - St. Anthony of the Desert

Anyone who knows me knows that I am an introvert and not just an introvert but extremely introverted. When I was in high school, my dream was to become a hermit. I wanted my own cabin somewhere in which I lived a self-sustaining life as much as possible.

This was long before computers and cell phones although I did have an electric typewriter. Then I went to college and wondered about becoming a nun, realizing I would probably enjoy some community.

And then I met Frank and an entirely different life blossomed before me. But I was still an introvert—I still needed time alone, time to sit in silence. I also still needed community as we are created for it. Over the years, that has worked itself out in various ways. When we worked at the

Warner Robins Daily Sun community meant getting together with co-workers occasionally for a meal or to play pool or spending time with family. This was also true when we worked for the *Rome News-Tribune*.

On the Appalachian Trail, we spent a lot of time hiking alone; in fact, we didn't really run into anybody for the first couple of months on the Trail. Later, there was a group of us that hiked together but separately so that most nights some part of that group would be together at a shelter or campsite.

And as the years flew by, community was found in family friends, work friends, church friends, and most importantly, for me, in the spiritual companions I found when I joined the Third Order, Society of Saint Francis.

An important part of our "Obedience" is to be involved in a "Fellowship," which is a gathering of Franciscans whether they be in the process toward profession or professed for many years. Meetings can be as often as monthly or quarterly, depending on the convenience for those attending. As *Forming the Life of a Franciscan* notes:

> "Francis attracted others to himself as soon as he began to live a life of total dedication to the love of Jesus. Like Jesus, he found brothers and sisters who wanted to walk with him in the Gospel way. Longing often for a life of solitude devoted entirely to prayer, Francis found community a mixed blessing. His brothers and sisters often disappointed him; they brought him both joy and grief."

Community is one of our obligations as tertiaries, and why

it is an important part of the process toward profession. But community is work. When I was in the process, I was limited to attending the annual meetings of the Southeast Convocation, which usually were held in Atlanta. There, I met Franciscans from all over the south but to be truthful, I usually avoided the social hours after dinner and spent the remainder of the evening in the quiet of my room.

For a number of years after I professed, I was involved in a Fellowship that took place in Athens, Georgia. That was a five-hour-plus drive from our home in Saint Marys, four from Savannah. It used to take three professed Tertiaries to form a Fellowship and at the time, I was able to be that third Tertiary. Fellowship meetings are times of being together as a family rather than 'meetings' in that sense of the term. Community worship, catching up on each other's lives, and talking about Franciscan books or the like as well as a shared meal are all part of a Fellowship meeting.

I hoped to make things a bit easier on myself by suggesting that we meet once a year closer to me—perhaps at Trinity in Statesboro or another church south of Athens. But that was out of range for a number of our members, and instead, I received permission to be a solitary Tertiary. I still took part in whatever meetings or events I could, but my 'solitariness' lasted about a decade.

Things changed again in 2023 when Frank entered the process to become a Franciscan Tertiary and we attended a General Convocation meeting in Scottsdale, Arizona, where we met together and in small groups with Tertiaries from all

Encountering the risen Jesus

Victoria's view of a Eucharist during the TSSF General Convocation at the Franciscan Renewal Center in Scottsdale, Arizona.

over the Americas—Canada, the U.S., Central, and South America.

When we returned to Savannah, we contacted some local-ish Tertiaries and we all agreed that it would be nice to start a new Fellowship made up of those in the process and those professed from South Carolina and Georgia. A few months in, we were joined by someone from Alabama. While the Sister Simplicity Fellowship mostly meets monthly by Zoom, we meet in person twice a year—once in Charleston in the Spring and Savannah in the Autumn. It is always joyful to get together with fellow Franciscans.

Holy Mysteries

Even as finding Christ in our brothers and sisters is part of our Franciscan journey, we learn from each other and share each other's joys and sorrows. As Jesus walked in a community of disciples who broke his heart through betrayal, denial and misunderstanding, so we too walk in a community of love with those who will disappoint and puzzle us, but also love us more than we deserve. Jesus defined the relationship that we ought to have with our community: we are to be a servant to all.

While I will still, and always, need my quiet/alone time, I will never underestimate the value of Christian community. It is important to be in community with fellow Christians whether it be in church or within a group in one's church, in a Cursillo Ultreya group, or a religious order. It seems particularly important in a rapidly growing secular world that we hold on to and learn to become community with those in our church homes.

As Richard Rohr noted, "St. Augustine said something quite shocking but surely true: 'The church is precisely the state of communion of the whole world.'" And if we can't find community in our churches then we can't share that connection with the world.

- What group have you been a part of that offered you this sense of close community?

Encountering the risen Jesus
Wednesday – The Strong Net

"After these things Jesus showed himself again to the disciples by the Sea of Tiberias; and he showed himself in this way. Gathered there together were Simon Peter, Thomas called the Twin, Nathanael of Cana in Galilee, the sons of Zebedee, and two others of his disciples. Simon Peter said to them, 'I am going fishing.' They said to him, 'We will go with you.' They went out and got into the boat, but that night they caught nothing. Just after daybreak, Jesus stood on the beach; but the disciples did not know that it was Jesus. Jesus said to them, 'Children, you have no fish, have you?' They answered him, 'No.' He said to them, 'Cast the net to the right side of the boat, and you will find some.' So they cast it, and now they were not able to haul it in because there were so many fish. That disciple whom Jesus loved said to Peter, 'It is the Lord!' When Simon Peter heard that it was the Lord, he put on some clothes, for he was naked, and jumped into the lake. But the other disciples came in the boat, dragging the net full of fish, for they were not far from the land, only about a hundred yards off. When they had gone ashore, they saw a charcoal fire there, with fish on it, and bread. Jesus said to them, 'Bring some of the fish that you have just caught.' So Simon Peter went aboard and hauled the net ashore, full of large fish, a hundred and fifty-three of them; and though there were so many, the net was not torn." (John 21:1-11)

Jesus finds his disciples in an unexpected place after his resurrection. They are not on the road proclaiming the word of God or baptizing. Rather, they have turned back to what they were doing before meeting Jesus—fishing. Perhaps that is why these men who were told to become fishers of people are now unsuccessful at fishing for fish.

From the shore, which is not far away, a man tells them to try casting their net on the right side of the boat. Unbelievably, they do as they are told. Maybe they were shrugging and rolling their eyes, and thinking, 'better placate the crazy person.' But a miracle occurs. There are so many fish that they cannot haul in the net. As they are struggling with the great catch, John suddenly realizes who it is and says to Peter, "It is the Lord!" Once they make it back to shore, we are told that they have caught large fish, 153 of them.

That seems like a rather specific and random amount. 153 fish. Really? Who counted them?

The great commentator on scripture, Jerome, offered a different possibility. Jerome, known mostly for translating the Bible into Latin (the Vulgate) cites a source that says the Greeks said there are 153 species of fish. If that is correct, the number could be symbolic of what is happening on the beach that morning. The disciples did not just catch fish, they caught big ones.

And not just big ones, but 153 different kinds of fish. It is the fish story version of the line from Revelation that says, "You ransomed for God saints from every tribe and language and people and nation."

John, in telling this story, has looked ahead to the time

when followers of Jesus would be preaching and teaching long after his resurrection and ascension. John didn't see a shore lined with dying fish, but a church full of people scooped up to safety after having found themselves lost in the chaos of the deep. John tells us that it will take all kinds to bring in the reign of God. There is no us and them in this story—it is all of us, together in one strong net.

Christians don't have inherently easier lives with no rough spots. Following Jesus won't prevent us from having a car wreck or cancer. What Jesus is illustrating through the 153 varieties of fish is that the Kingdom of God is for all the peoples of the earth. And, even better, the net woven from God's grace and love is big enough to hold us all without tearing. And in that net, we find the strength to carry us through the hardest of times.

We have hope in the God who goes to the depths of human existence to love those who see themselves as lost, unfit, and sinful as well as those who are trying their best to live out their Baptismal vows. Fortunately, God is always offering a chance for a clean slate, a fresh start. God will never leave us to the chaos that threatens to consume us. God will cast a net.

- Has there ever been a time when you needed the net of God's love and grace?
- Have you ever offered that same love and grace to someone who desperately needed it?

Holy Mysteries
THURSDAY – QUOTATION

Holy Sonnet 14

Batter my heart, three-person'd God, for you
As yet but knock, breathe, shine, and seek to mend;
That I may rise and stand, o'erthrow me, and bend
Your force to break, blow, burn, and make me new.
I, like an usurp'd town to another due,
Labor to admit you, but oh, to no end;
Reason, your viceroy in me, me should defend,
But is captiv'd, and proves weak or untrue.
Yet dearly I love you, and would be lov'd fain,
But am betroth'd unto your enemy;
Divorce me, untie or break that knot again,
Take me to you, imprison me, for I,
Except you enthrall me, never shall be free,
Nor ever chaste, except you ravish me.

-John Donne (1572–1631), *Holy Sonnets*

Known for surprising imagery in his poetry, John Donne offers a collision of martial and marital images. The language one came to expect in Donne's love poetry is put to a very different use. This sonnet addressed to the Holy Trinity is a prayer for Divine forcefulness to break through the poet's defenses as he, like a town taken by enemy forces, has been taken over by the evil one. In a time of doubt and uncertainty, when his own reason fails to point him to the

Encountering the risen Jesus

Holy Trinity, Donne cries out asking God to go on the offensive to reclaim the enemy territory within his own will. In an opening quatrain filled with action in piling on verbs, he prays "bend your force to break, blow, burn, and make me new." Donne asks God to resurrect his faith. Then he ends with the line that would have been shocking in a "Holy Sonnet," in writing, "Nor ever chaste, except you ravish me."

- What stands out for you in the poem's symbolism?
- When have you wished the Holy Spirit would cut out being coy and make the divine self known so clearly to you that you could not help but believe?

FRIDAY – FRANK'S REFLECTION

There is no hurt like church hurt, where one is wounded by the place where we should find healing. In my role in assisting Bishop Scott Benhase as Canon to the Ordinary, I came in on a couple of occasions right after congregations had a split with many or even most members leaving to found a church in the Anglican Church in North America (ACNA) denomination.

The pain in a community divided over the issues of the day is deep and lasting, but not beyond God's power to redeem and heal. So perhaps, it should be expected that my most meaningful Easter came together right on the heels of a painful church split. Bishop Benhase and I met with the vestry at Calvary in Americus and it was clear that the Rector and the majority of the vestry were deeply displeased as the bishop had not sided with the priest in excommunicating two parishioners over a dispute about the books a book club group would read as they were not explicitly Christian works. They also cited a litany of quotations from sermons and other writings by some bishops in the church and the then Presiding Bishop given as evidence of the Episcopal Church not taking scripture seriously. The commitment to faith in Jesus Christ that Bishop Benhase and I have did not seem to matter in the meeting.

Yet, I was still quite surprised when a Calvary parishioner who was a reporter for the local paper called to say she saw the Junior Warden in a storefront space that looked like a church. She stopped and went in and he would not talk to her at all, but she got the name of the new ACNA congregation off the building permit posted on the door. I checked the Secretary of State website and learned that the wardens and the congregation's largest donor had formed the corporation days after that meeting with the vestry. The Bishop sent a letter via email to the vestry letting them know that all who could still sign that declaration required of vestry members in diocesan canons were still the vestry of Calvary. Any who could not were asked to step down. The declaration, is similar to one required of clergy in ordination, says:

> "I do believe that the Holy Scriptures contain all Doctrine required as necessary for eternal salvation through faith in Jesus Christ, and I do yield my hearty assent and approbation to the doctrine,

worship, and discipline of The Episcopal Church; and I promise that I will faithfully execute the office of Vestry Member or Warden of Calvary Parish in Sumter County, according to my best knowledge and skill."

The diocesan Chancellor, the Rev. Jim Elliott, was closer and he drove to the church to meet any remaining vestry and found nine departing members of vestry assisting the priest in moving out of his office. It was agreed that I would work to keep their Holy Week schedule and I asked the Rev. Kedron Jarvis Nicholson to assist me. We had been in seminary together and she had moved to Dawson for her husband to work in the family's business. On Palm Sunday, she celebrated and I preached and then Kedron took over the daily services Monday through Friday. On Saturday, we would hold the Great Vigil of Easter. Kedron and I worked with the church' leaders to plan the liturgy. We would begin as night fell in the garden alongside the church where parishioners are buried, then move to the parish hall, and end in the church.

Driving over from Savannah, I recalled that I had not secured tapers for the candlelit portion. I called the Rev. Jim Clendinen who was then serving at Annunciation in Vidalia. I drove through the parking lot of that church on the way and he handed off the candles without me or Victoria getting out of the car. We arrived in Americus in time to collect wood for the new fire that begins the Great Vigil. We got everything set up in time. The fire was kindled, we lit the tapers, and

Holy Mysteries

*The Easter Vigil 2012 at Calvary in Americus in 2012
that Frank describes in his reflection.*

we processed into the darkness of the parish hall as if early Christians entering the catacombs to pray. There in the soft glow of the many lit tapers, one well-read story after another recounted salvation history. As we reached the turning point in the liturgy to Easter we entered the beautifully decorated church and the lights came on as we proclaimed alleluia, alleluia, alleluia.

Words fail to capture the joy of that evening, but it certainly gets at what we mean by the holy mystery of participation. We were deeply connected to each other and to the Holy Trinity who was with us. My best self prays that that same God was equally present to the newly born

ACNA congregation, as the joy I felt was not of triumphing over anyone or anything. I sensed that God had not left us comfortless, but had come in the power of the Holy Spirit. There is no joy like church joy as it is a joy experienced in close community. The barely remembered candles, the fire that came together at the last second, and the beautifully read scripture was part of it, but mostly the feeling was that of the presence of the living God.

- When have you known that you were taking part in something bigger than yourself?

Saturday – Breakfast on the Beach

"Jesus said to them, 'Come and have breakfast.' Now none of the disciples dared to ask him, 'Who are you?' because they knew it was the Lord. Jesus came and took the bread and gave it to them, and did the same with the fish. This was now the third time that Jesus appeared to the disciples after he was raised from the dead." (John 21:12-14)

After filling their net, Jesus invites his disciples to breakfast. John seems to need to clarify that by this point, they all knew they were experiencing the risen Lord even though most of them had seen the risen Jesus twice already. Yet, even so, Jesus must feed his disciples again. And just as with the thousands on the hillside, he treats them to bread and fish. If the fish filling the net were not enough to break through the disorientation of his death, Jesus decides he must make the message even clearer in cooking them a meal and eating with them.

It's just like old times—sharing a meal together, falling easily into camaraderie—the hard part would have been leaving the beach. They must have been thinking, "Couldn't life always be like this? What more could we need?" For the disciples, the answer could have easily been: "Nothing. We don't need anything more."

But that's not what Jesus wanted. That's not why he spent several years of his life teaching these guys and giving his life for the world. Jesus desperately wanted more. He wanted every single person in creation to hear his words and take them to heart.

Yet, if the disciples of Jesus had stayed on the beach, then the Good News of Christianity would never have reached us. Jesus longed for a relationship with all that he had made and the way to get it was for these guys around the campfire to get going. Never again would they have that easy fellowship of breakfast on the beach. But Jesus never promised them that it would be easy.

Their tightly woven Christian community was about to acquire a lot more strands—people who were nothing like them. People like the Greek, Stephen, who had never been a Jew yet could preach a moving sermon on Abraham. People like Saul, who while in the midst of hunting them down and murdering the followers of this new Way, would be called by Jesus to join their community. Soon there would be a lot more people in their nets and these people would bring change to the camaraderie they felt that morning with Jesus.

But Jesus did not teach us to remain in our church homes comfortable with our camaraderie, pushing newcomers away by making them feel they are not one of 'us', even if done unintentionally. In addition to loving God and loving ourselves, Jesus also taught us to love our neighbors as ourselves.

We know that what we do have as followers of Jesus is to develop a relationship with the God who is working to redeem our world, one precious life at a time. What we have is the knowledge that everything we now experience is not all there is. We have the hope in the God who goes to the depths of human existence to love those who see themselves as lost, unfit, and sinful. God is always offering us a chance for a clean slate, a fresh start. Just as Jesus did with his disciples. When they tried to return to their previous lives, fishing for fish, he appeared to them and reminded them that they were called to be fishers of men.

It happens again and again. We find a church that makes us feel as if we have found a family and that is great. But what happens when someone new wants to join the family? Do you welcome them with open arms or are you just polite and secretly hope that they will not return?

- Have you ever felt called to do something but find that fear or complacency makes it easier to remain with the status quo?

Holy Mysteries

Boticelli's The Last Communion of Saint Jerome (Early 1490s)

Encountering the risen Jesus
Sunday – Participation Revisited

> "'Love is stronger than death' is the message of Easter."
> -Richard Rohr

We were created to share in God's love—for Him, for ourselves, and for each other. God became flesh to remind us of this, then God as human died so that we could share this wondrous news with all of humanity. In addition, we should be worshipping weekly in the remembrance of God and what God has done for us by attending a church service or services and sharing that remembrance with other Christians.

Anamnesis is the Greek word for "remember" used in the liturgies in which we recall the Passion, Death, Resurrection, and Ascension of Jesus. It originated in the words (from the Greek) that Jesus used during the Last Supper, "Do this in memory of me" in Luke 22:19 as well as 1 Corinthians 11:24-25. It is a key concept in liturgical theology. In worship, we recall God's saving deeds. This memorial aspect is not just a passive process but part of how we participate in the divine life as we actually enter into the Paschal mystery.

Another way to put it is that *anamnesis* is un-amnesia or more simply, remembrance is an unforgetting of something already known. In that sense, we are all beloved children of God, loved by our creator who created us out of love for love. We were formed to love God with all our heart, mind, soul, and strength, and to love our neighbors as ourselves. But in a world turned from God it is easy to forget that we are known and loved. However, in the Eucharist we remember,

Holy Mysteries

or in this case, un-forget the central truth that God made us out of love for love and wants so much better for us than the mess we can, and usually do, make of our lives. God, the Holy Trinity, will never leave us or forsake us. This is what many Christians never forgot in the persecutions of the early church: they were steadfast in their faith and belief that they were members of the Body of Christ and, after death, they would be remembered.

Dismember can mean to have an arm or a leg or other body part, amputated and this brings us closer to what is meant here. When a surgeon operates to reattach that body part, they are re-membering the person, adding that member back to the body. That is what is meant when 'do this in remembrance of me' is spoken during the Eucharist. It is re-membering or bringing the Body of Christ together.

When we partake of the Eucharist, we are reminded of whose we are, and we are knit back together as a Body. The real work of remembering is Christ's work in us by the power of the Holy Spirit. The world wants us to forget our identity in Christ. The world wants to tell you that you are not enough—thin enough, smart enough, young enough, mature enough, famous enough, rich enough, good enough, powerful enough, deserving enough. Yet in Christ we find that we are always enough because Jesus loves us as we are and the God who made us knows us fully, loves us completely, and will never forget us. Even someone with dementia who is losing a sense of themselves, remains whole within the divine life in which we participate as we are always remembered in the heart of God.

Encountering the risen Jesus

As baptized Christians, we all share a common call to continue in the Apostles' teaching and to proclaim by word and example the Good News of God in Christ as we seek and serve Christ in all persons and respect the dignity of every human being. In this, we take up the common call we share with those first followers of Jesus who lived boldly into their faith in a risen savior. Even as many converts heard the lions roaring as they waited to be led to their deaths in the Coliseum, they were still able to sing hymns of praise joyfully.

We are empowered by the same Holy Spirit that is within us, the same Holy Spirit that has spoken to the hearts of Christians throughout the centuries, the Holy Spirit that lets us all know that we participate in the divine life as we have been re-membered by Christ.

In whatever we face, God is with us. Nothing can stop God's love for us. Every time we hear the stories of God's saving acts, we must remember who we are as we share in the body and blood of Christ. Remember that we are being strengthened to be Christ's body in the world. Jesus passed from death to life to show us the Way through faith in him, and nothing, not even death, can ever remove God's love for you.

"Everyone who loves is born of God and knows God, Anyone who fails to love can never have known God, for God is love." (1 John 4:8)

- How do you experience the Eucharist? Do you ever feel re-membered?

Week VI
Sacramentality

Monday – Introducing Sacramentality

"We are not to restrict God's presence in the world
to a limited range of 'pious' objects and situations,
while labeling everything else as 'secular';
but we are to see all things as essentially sacred,
as a gift from God and a means of communion with him."

-Kallistos Ware, *The Orthodox Way*

Informed by last week's devotions on our participating in the life of the Trinity, we move into sacramentality. Within our Anglican tradition, we find that faith and reason are not seen as separate or opposed, in the same way that we see no sharp division between the sacred and the secular. We live in a world hallowed by the presence of God in which the natural world and other people alike can and do convey something of that divine presence. This means that the creation can be a "sacrament," an outward and visible sign, of God.

By taking the word sacrament in its broadest sense, as meaning the visible sign of something sacred that remains hidden, we could say that the whole world is sacramental. It would mean that material things are, as seen by humankind, the signs of things that are spiritual and sacred. The flowers near the altar, the people in the pews, the bread and wine of Eucharist, the birds at the feeder, houseplants, the fish in the aquarium . . . I could go on and on . . . are all sacramental. Because sacramentality is the principle that says everything in creation—living creatures, places, the environment, and even the universe itself—can reveal God. It is under this principle that the division between sacred and secular is erased: Everything carries the potential to reveal the holy, because everything comes from the same source, in the Holy Trinity.

There is an important distinction to make here that we find in the writings of William Temple, who held the highest two positions in the Church of England in an important point in more recent history. As the Archbishop of York from 1929-1942 and then the Archbishop of Canterbury in 1945, he was a renowned scholar who became a national and international leader in the ecumenical movement. In a series of lectures "Nature, Man, and God" he had given from 1932-1934, Temple spoke of the Sacramental Universe. In a lecture by this title he wrote of faith and reason saying, "the progress towards truth in religion and in science follows converging lines. We serve truth as a whole most effectively, not when we seek to impose religious ideas upon science, nor when we seek to impose scientific ideas upon religion, but when studying both religion and the physical world with open and unprejudiced minds we seek to read their lesson."

In the Incarnation, God becoming human in Jesus, we see the Holy Trinity entering into the creation in a way that revealed the spiritual and the material could be united. Temple said later in this lecture on the Sacramental Universe that the world, "which is the self-expressive utterance of the Divine Word, becomes itself a true revelation" as "what comes is not truth concerning God, but God Himself."

The corrective here is that material would, can, and does reveal something of the divine. Yet we know that Jesus, the Incarnate Word, is the ultimate sacrament through which we see all sacramental reality most clearly. What we glimpse imperfectly through the material world, we see revealed fully in Jesus. His life and ministry, his death and resurrection, his sending the Holy Spirit as a comforter and advocate, give us the best lens through which to see the world and our place in it rightly. As the Apostle Paul wrote, "For it is God who said, 'Let light shine out of the darkness,' who has shone in our hearts to give the light of the knowledge of the glory of God in the face of Jesus Christ" (II Corinthians 4:6).

For Temple, Natural Theology, which relied on what we learn from the creation alone without the specific revelation of the Incarnation, "ends in a hunger which it cannot satisfy" as "the arch falls for lack of its keystone and the gulf between mind and the universe in which it appears remains unbridged." Jesus provides that bridge between the sacramental universe in which we live and the Holy Trinity that is its source and its end.

In coming to see that we live within a sacramental universe, we are given eyes to see that the whole creation is shot through with the presence of God. Then we can find the providence of God in the creation, as the earth tends to bring forth what we need to sustain us. We see the grace of God in the rain falling on the just and the unjust. We can come to see the face of Christ in other people as the God who needs nothing gives us the gift of neighbors in need to whom we can share the love we have for our creator and sustainer.

- Temple believed creation is sacramental. What parts of creation are most sacramental/holy for you?
- When was the last time you were doing something in your daily life that you felt a connection to God and creation?

Holy Mysteries
Tuesday – Victoria's Reflection

"… scientists now tell us that all light in the universe
is electromagnetically connected and
that all natural light is in fact one.
The Risen Christ is the personification of
this one Light that includes all light,
which is why he is always described as 'dazzling white'
or 'like lightning'." (Matthew 28:3)

-Richard Rohr, *Immortal Diamond*

In the first week of this devotional, I named how I came to see the Shroud of Turin as a sacred relic despite the evidence that pointed to its being a much later artifact. After reading the article that disappointed me, I had the serendipity of finding two pencils—one, a small red pencil that had *Time* magazine printed on it; the other, a white pencil with the names of the books of the New Testament printed on it. I didn't talk about this incident that felt to me like confirmation. I read numerous books and articles on the Shroud and joined the website, shroud.com, so that I would receive updates about it. I corresponded with Barrie Schwortz, the official photographer for the 1978 Shroud study that produced the images I first saw in Atlanta. I also purchased a few images, myself. Schwortz created and was admin for the shroud.com site for nearly 30 years. Sadly, as I was starting to work on this reflection, I received the news that Barrie Schwortz had passed away after a short illness.

Despite the carbon dating result, my conviction that the Shroud was real has remained firm. The BBC News Magazine wrote an article in 2015 that said, "According to an international team of scientists and other interested folk called the Yahoo Shroud Science Group, hypotheses about the genesis of the shroud 'involving the Resurrection of Jesus of Nazareth cannot be rejected'". Among them, the group members write, "are hypotheses correlated to an energy source coming from the enveloped or wrapped Man, [and] others correlated to surface electrostatic discharges caused by an electric field. Since these hypotheses appear to invoke processes unknown to science, which presumably occur during a return from the dead, it's technically true that science can't disprove them - nor really say anything about them at all."

William West wrote:

> "I spent five years researching my recently-published book *Riddles of the Shroud: Questions Science Can't Answer*, and the evidence suggests the Shroud covered Jesus at the point of resurrection.
>
> The evidence is so strong that it is hard to imagine anyone with an open mind seeing it as anything less than compelling. Despite the fact that most people seem to think research on the Shroud came to an end with the carbon dating in 1988, it has become the most researched single artifact in history. The bottom line is that science has shown the image on

the cloth is an 'impossible' image – one that cannot be replicated. One of the main reasons is, as scientists have now confirmed, the image on the Shroud had to be caused by a mysterious burst of light – that is, electromagnetic radiation.

In short, the evidence indicates the Shroud was wrapped around a real body that simply 'dematerialised' without disturbing the perfectly formed blood clots on the cloth. That could only happen through an event like that described in the Gospels as the resurrection – an event that, as the Gospels state, freed Jesus' body from material constraints."

Vindication arrived this year as new scientific tests conducted on the Shroud of Turin have revealed that the flax used to make the linen was grown in the Middle East. The results of isotope tests provide new evidence that the shroud is the actual garment that was used to cover the body of Jesus Christ following his crucifixion – and is not a forgery that was created in medieval Europe. Fragments of cloth taken from the shroud show that its flax originated in the western Levant, a swathe of land occupied today by Israel, Lebanon and western parts of Jordan and Syria.

A scholar renowned for his books on the life of Jesus, Jean-Christian Petitfils told the *National Catholic Register* of how close examination of the shroud points to facts about the crucifixion including the body being flogged very violently, in the Roman way, and not in the Jewish way, with

Encountering the risen Jesus

a flagrum, which had two small balls and a barbell between them, the trace of which can be seen under a microscope. He said there is evidence of Jesus being speared in his side that reveals the type of Roman spear used. Looking at the accurate details seen in the relic, Petitfils said, "The examination of the Shroud leads us inevitably to the mystery of the Resurrection, although this burial cloth is not in itself a proof of the Resurrection, which can only be experienced and understood through faith. But it does give us some very unsettling clues."

And yet, as satisfying as this proof is, it still does not remove the mystery of the Shroud for me. While we can guess at what happened, I don't believe we will ever actually know and thus the Shroud will remain clouded by mystery as God is shrouded by mystery.

- Something that proves the presence and power of God may not speak to another person. What do you point to as one of the reasons why you believe?

WEDNESDAY – FEED MY SHEEP

"When they had finished breakfast, Jesus said to Simon Peter, 'Simon son of John, do you love me more than these?' He said to him, 'Yes, Lord; you know that I love you.' Jesus said to him, 'Feed my lambs.' A second time he said to him, 'Simon son of John, do you love me?' He said to him, 'Yes, Lord; you know that I love you.' Jesus said to him, 'Tend my sheep.' He said to him the third time, 'Simon son of John, do you love me?' Peter felt hurt because he said to him the third time, 'Do you love me?' And he said to him, 'Lord, you know everything; you know that I love you.' Jesus said to him, 'Feed my sheep. Very truly, I tell you, when you were younger, you used to fasten your own belt and to go wherever you wished. But when you grow old, you will stretch out your hands, and someone else will fasten a belt around you and take you where you do not wish to go.' (He said this to indicate the kind of death by which he would glorify God.) After this he said to him, 'Follow me.'" (John 21:15-19)

When Jesus pulls Simon Peter aside and asks him, "Simon, son of John, do you love me?", it is the third time he has appeared to the remaining eleven after being raised from the dead. On this third appearance, he eats a breakfast of bread and fish with them. Right afterwards, he takes Peter away from the others, although I am sure they are being watched by at least a few of the disciples, as Jesus gives his 'Rock' some final instructions.

But Jesus doesn't ask Peter only once if he loves Him. He asks three times. It seems clear that this is a chance for Peter to redeem himself for having denied Jesus three times before His death. It is difficult to believe that wasn't what was on Peter's mind as he answered for the third time, because he is hurt when Jesus asks the question a third time.

Jesus is rounding up one more lost sheep in letting his friend, Simon Peter, affirm his love before calling to him

Encountering the risen Jesus

once more saying, "Follow me." Peter will continue to walk in Jesus' ways being faithful to death as he was hung on a cross. Peter said that he wasn't worthy to die like Jesus and at his own request was crucified upside down. But in the decades before that last act of devotion, Simon Peter shared the mercy and forgiveness he found in that stroll on the beach. Peter wanted everyone to experience that same love of God.

We too know that the love of God is not supposed to be like a pocket warmer, that keeps you warm while leaving others out in the cold. Jesus did not teach us to just love God and love ourselves, though that is two thirds of what he said. Jesus also taught us to love our neighbors as ourselves.

We have hope in the God who goes to the depths of human existence to love, truly love, those who see themselves as lost, unfit, and sinful. God is always offering a chance for a clean slate, a fresh start, and will never leave you to the chaos that threatens to consume you. God will send a net.

God knows you fully, loves you unreservedly, and wants better for you. God wants the same for others in your life. And when you invite them to join you in worship in your church, you are not trying to grow a church, but throwing your friend a lifeline. And you can be sure that your congregation is one where they will be welcomed and loved by the congregation and by the host of our feast, who is Jesus.

We don't have to have all the answers to share God's love for what we do have as followers of Jesus in a relationship with the God who is working to redeem our world one wild and precious life at a time. We have the knowledge that everything we now see and experience is not all there is. The creator of the cosmos knows you by name, has always loved you, will never give up on you even if you deny him, and wants better for you.

- Jesus asked Peter the question three times. Have you ever had to prove your love for something or someone more than once?

Thursday – Quotation

And truly, I reiterate,.. nothing's small!
No lily-muffled hum of a summer-bee,
But finds some coupling with the spinning stars;
No pebble at your foot, but proves a sphere;
No chaffinch, but implies the cherubim:
And, — glancing on my own thin, veined wrist, —
In such a little tremour of the blood
The whole strong clamour of a vehement soul
Doth utter itself distinct. Earth's crammed with heaven,
And every common bush afire with God:
But only he who sees, takes off his shoes,
The rest sit round it, and pluck blackberries,
And daub their natural faces unaware
More and more, from the first similitude.

-Elizabeth Barrett Browning (1806-1861), from *Aurora Leigh: Book 7*

Encountering the risen Jesus

Revered for her verse, Elizabeth Barrett Browning (1806-1861) was a poet of such renown that she was considered for Poet Laureate on the death of Wordsworth in 1850. Though that post would go to Tennyson, the pause to consider her shows the critical esteem Elizabeth had already garnered. Robert Browning came to know Elizabeth's poetry first and she his. There followed a courtship carried out in 575 letters exchanged across two years before the pair eloped. They moved to Italy, settling in Florence, where Elizabeth was the draw that brought a steady stream of readers from across Europe and the United States to their parlor. Their son, Robert, was born there in 1849.

We see her influence on the English poets of the 1800s in the reclusive Emily Dickinson keeping a framed portrait of Barret Browning in her bedroom in Amherst, Massachusetts. Dickinson's life had been transformed by the poetry of 'that Foreign Lady.' Emily saw in Elizabeth a woman who proved what was possible to achieve through the power of the written word. Within her body of work, she addressed social injustices including child labor in mills and in mines throughout England, the slave trade, the confines life placed on women in society, the oppressive rule of Austria over the people of Italy.

Even Barrett Browning's sacramental understanding of life was a natural part of who she was; it was part of the very essence of her life. She was the eldest of twelve children whose parents' wealth came from the plantations they owned in Jamaica. Her mother died when she was about twenty two. She suffered from poor health most of her life—injuring her spine at fifteen, bursting a blood vessel in her chest that made her health even more fragile. Steeped in religion as people were at the time, she, like other writers and poets, often mentioned God in her works. In this excerpt from her verse novel Aurora Leigh, the poet offers these lines about the divine presence within creation.

- Have you ever 'taken off your shoes' because you were overwhelmed by the sacredness of something?
- Are you more taken by things naturally created like birds or flowers or do man-made creations like architecture, music, and art inspire you more?

Friday – Frank's Reflection

Walking beneath a canopy of redwoods towering 300 feet above the trail puts oneself in perspective. Vastly larger and immensely older than the hikers they dwarf, the giant trees evoke a sense of wonder. We hiked under the evergreens along Prairie Creek Trail with a small group of family and friends in March 2023. The hike under the towering trunks and overhanging branches was like walking through a vast natural cathedral. We almost experienced awe fatigue as each turn in the trail revealed yet another breathtaking scene. And yet, that sense of reverence remained with every fresh vista.

The next day, the same group gathered under a redwood on another trail in Redwood National Park during a break in

Encountering the risen Jesus

Frank officiates Griffin and Chaz' wedding among the redwoods with Victoria and Griffin's best friend, Kalyn Baylis, in the background.

the nearly ever present rain. I officiated a simple Prayer Book service as our daughter, Griffin, and her husband, Chaz, were united in the sacrament of marriage. That evening, the thirteen of us present for the joyous occasion made tacos and fixings together and sat down to eat. Each of these three events–the walk beneath the redwoods, the wedding, and the meal–were uniquely moving experiences.

The two sacraments instituted by Jesus, baptism and Eucharist, are described in the catechism in the Book of Common Prayer together with the five additional sacramental rites of confirmation, ordination, holy matrimony, reconciliation of a penitent, and unction. Beyond these rites, we know that our experience of the divine is not limited to what happens in church. We can know the grace of the ordinary as we sometimes feel the presence of God, the Holy Trinity, in the mundane stuff of our daily life, as the whole creation is shot through with the presence of God.

The Russian Orthodox theologian Alexander Schmemann wrote in *For the Life of the World*, "The world is a fallen world because it has fallen away from the awareness that God is all in all. The accumulation of this disregard for God is the original sin that blights the world." Seeing that God is in all is one of the many places in which the churches of the east and west are united. The most amazing part of this is that it need not have been so. God did not need the creation, but chose to create the cosmos and everything in it, from the startlingly bright red eft newts I enjoy spotting on rainy hikes in the Great Smokies to the wildebeests I have watched migrate across the savanna in Tanzania. God did not need us or the redwoods or the vast nebulae in space and yet the Trinity of persons did create everything out of love for love, and the interconnections we share with one another and all creation are more important than what separates us.

The French Eastern Orthodox theologian Olivier Clément said, "True mysticism is to discover the extraordinary in the ordinary." I have been aided in this by Dacher Keltner's book *Awe: The New Science of Everyday Wonder and How It Can Transform Your Life*. His look at the science behind awe left me reflecting on the everyday experiences of wonder that we would do well to notice as they open us up to connections that matter. When you are in the presence of something vast that expands your understanding of the world, it takes your breath away. You are overwhelmed by a sense that there is more to life than seemed possible until that moment. For God is present in these everyday epiphanies. Keltner defines eight larger categories of experience that can generate awe: moral beauty, collective effervescence, nature, music, visual design, spiritual awe, life and death, and epiphanies.

The hike, wedding, and meal I began this reflection with combined the collective effervescence, which is how he describes a deep sense of a collective self experienced as "we" and "us" in the midst of nature in an experience that was spiritual. Small wonder that I found that event an ever-unfolding sense of wow. I didn't cry, even though I am given to tears on occasion. But I was amazed at the sense that there is more to life than what we experience in most moments.

In making the faith of the church our own, we have not just the text of a book or the traditions of the church, but we too have experiences that there is something so much more than the rational mind can convey, expressing a truth of scope that is so much more than ordinary logic or reason. This is because we experience not just the natural world, in which we do see God, but we also have these transcendent experiences as well where it feels like the veil between heaven and earth is pulled back just a bit.

I will never get over our daughter, Griffin's, birth at home with a midwife. It was, like most births, difficult and took many more hours than we wished, but it was beautiful in its own way as well, and I saw such strength in Victoria and vulnerability in our newborn girl. I thought there could be nothing more wonderful than Victoria and I looking into her eyes. Then in time as she came to know and love us, there was so much more. I sat with seven-year old Griffin on the edge of the Grand Canyon and felt the rush of the wind wash over us. And I have known the power of her forgiveness when I took a wrong turn in parenting. While my relationship with her is unique, I could name the many other ways in which I have experienced that something more in so many relationships.

These experiences connect us to each other even as they connect us with the divine. The Holy Trinity is the transcendent one, present in all creation and also breaking into creation taking our breath away with moments that reveal that there is more to life than seemed possible until that epiphany. These are glimpses at a creation packed with the presence of the creator.

- When have you experienced a sense of collective, a we or us, that felt like something so much more?
- What takes your breath away? When have you known a little epiphany?

SATURDAY – THE GREAT COMMISSION

"Now the eleven disciples went to Galilee, to the mountain to which Jesus had directed them. When they saw him, they worshiped him; but some doubted. And Jesus came and said to them, 'All authority in heaven and on earth has been given to me. Go therefore and make disciples of all nations, baptizing them in the name of the Father and of the Son and of the Holy Spirit, and teaching them to obey everything that I have commanded you. And remember, I am with you always, to the end of the age.'" (Matthew 28:16-20)

This passage of Scripture, which concludes the Gospel of Matthew, resonates particularly to those called to Holy Orders. But were the eleven disciples the only ones on that mountain, or did the risen Jesus, as in life, draw a crowd? Whether it was 11 or 1,111, Jesus was urging all of his followers to fulfill this mission. This is not something for deacons, priests, and bishops alone, but for each of us who follow Jesus. Neither a great suggestion nor a simple invitation, in the Great Commission Jesus charges those who follow Him to take the Good News to the ends of the earth. "Go," Jesus tells us.

Yet, we can never give away what we don't possess ourselves. To make disciples, we have to be disciples. We can look to what Jesus taught about his expectation for those who followed him. Here are a handful of examples from the Gospels of Luke and John:

Jesus talks of the cost of discipleship in the 14th chapter of Luke's Gospel as he teaches that disciples are to have a holy detachment, not placing our essential hope or trust in anyone or anything other than God. He put this in a jarring way, "If anyone comes to me and does not hate father and mother, wife and children, brothers and sisters—yes, even their own life—such a person cannot be my disciple" (Luke 14:26). He added that we are also to die to ourselves saying, "Whoever does not carry the cross and follow me cannot be my disciple" (Luke 14:27). Jesus then added the things we own to the equation, "So therefore, none of you can become my disciple if you do not give up all your possessions" (Luke 14:33). The warning here is that if we put people or things ahead of him, we are making them into idols.

Jesus' friend John recorded how we must come to know and follow his teaching and all of scripture. "Then Jesus said to the Jews who had believed in him, 'If you continue in my word, you are truly my disciples,'" (John 8:31). Jesus called us to the same self-giving love he demonstrated as he talked to his disciples on the night before he died, "I give you a new commandment, that you love one another. Just as I have loved you, you also should love one another. By this everyone will know that you are my disciples, if you have love for one another" (John 13:34-35). Jesus asks us to love others with the same unconditional love he freely offers us. On that same night, Jesus told his followers, "If you abide in me and my words abide in you, ask for whatever you wish, and it will be done for you. My Father is glorified by this, that you bear much fruit and become my disciples" (John 15:7-8).

Paul listed the fruit of the Spirit to the Christians in Galatia as, "love, joy, peace, patience, kindness, goodness, faithfulness, and self-control" (Galatians 5:22-23). In calling us to bear much fruit as his disciples, Jesus is naming those qualities that we are to have and to offer to others as we make disciples.

- Some of the disciples doubted. You may have doubts and fears too. Can you be open with the Lord about them?
- What do you do to make the love of God present and real to those you meet?

Sunday – Sacramentality Revisited

Many peoples around the world have developed rituals that instill within the child the importance of coming-of-age or the religion into which they were born that are very different from our practices of baptism and confirmation.

Among the Sateré-Mawé people, indigenous to the Brazilian state of Amazonas, boys endure an initiation with bullet ants to mark their coming of age at 13. The boys search the jungle for bullet ants which are then sedated by an adult who submerges them in an herbal solution that anesthetizes them. The ants are then woven into mittens fashioned from leaves with the ants' stingers pointed inwards. As the ants wake up about an hour later, the initiation begins. Each boy must wear the ant gloves for ten full minutes as the angry ants inject him with neurotoxins. Justin Schmidt, who created a sting pain index, says that while the bullet ant sting is never fatal, it creates what he calls, "Pure, intense, brilliant pain." The intense pain lasts from 12-36 hours, giving the initiates ample opportunity to show they are ready for manhood. But the test is not a one time rite of passage as each teen endures this process about twenty times over the course of several months to complete the initiation.

In Malaysia, Muslim girls celebrate Khatam Al Koran on their eleventh birthday. This day is marked by a ritual that demonstrates their progress in learning to read and recite the Koran in a rite they have been preparing for since the age of four. Like Jewish children with a Bar or Bat Mitzvah, the girls study the Koran so that they can recite the final chapter of the sacred text in their local Mosque.

There is a custom among the Osage people that instills a child with the sacramentality of the world. When a child is born, a holy person is summoned to recite to the newborn infant the story of the creation of the world and of the animals that walk this planet. This is the very first act and must be completed before the baby is allowed to nurse. When the child is weaned from their mother's breast, a holy person is once again called for. This time, they tell the child a creation story that culminates in the sacred origins of water. Only then is the child given water to drink. Finally, as the child is ready to consume solid food, the process repeats with the holy person telling the origins of the grain and other food they will eat. The object of all of this is to introduce the maturing child to the sacramental reality of the world. This child grows up knowing that eating is a sacred act that connects us to creation as well as a physiological act.

Encountering the risen Jesus

These initiation rites of other cultures show a common human longing to mark important transitions in life, often in ways in which we prove ourselves worthy of the community. Our initiation rites are impoverished by comparison, largely as we have come to teach the faith increasingly less and less. The stories of the Bible are no longer common knowledge. As noted in the introduction, early Christianity involved steps taken to make sure that converts were truly devoted to Christ. Once Christians stopped meeting in private homes and synagogues and had their own buildings to worship in, about the third century, all transgressions were confessed before the congregation. The bishop would then apply different levels of temporary excommunication for each offense. Those undergoing penance were relegated to the vestibule. If they were still penitent, they would then be allowed to stand with the catechumens before they were once again admitted to the main body of the congregation, and finally restored to full communion.

The penitential process could take up to twenty years in the case of serious offenses. Some offenses were considered so serious that the person was permanently expelled from the church for life and only allowed to receive communion on their deathbeds. The excommunicated were known as 'weepers' and they were allowed to remain on the front steps of the church during the liturgy so that they could beg for the prayers of the faithful entering and leaving the building.

Also, for a very long time because of the fear of persecution, only baptized Christians in good standing were allowed to remain throughout the service. Non-Christians were escorted from the building after the Great Litany, and catechumens were escorted out before the consecration of the Eucharist.

It could also take anywhere from nine months to three years to convert to Christianity. While awaiting baptism, which was always deferred until Easter, one was designated a catechumen and had only limited access to the Scriptures or the Divine Liturgy. Only the baptized could read or hear the Gospels. Most of us are probably glad that we aren't forced to demonstrate that level of devotion anymore. And within the boundless grace of God we know that we do not have to prove ourselves worthy. Rather, we are to embrace the mercy of the God who loves us and wants better for us than the mess we humans can make of our lives. In capturing a new sense of sacramentality, God's presence all around us seeking to break through and reveal God's love for us, we can come to see how God loves us despite the ways we fall short.

In his book *Immortal Diamond*, Richard Rohr has an interesting suggestion: "Many Christians begin Lent on Ash Wednesday with the signing of ashes on their forehead and the words from Genesis 3:19," he says, but continues, "which is just the first shocking part of the message: "Dust you are, and to dust you shall return."

He says that we need to close the circle on Easter. "But then we should be anointed ('Christed') with holy oil on Easter morning with the other half of the message: "Love is always stronger than death, and unto that love you have now returned."

Encountering the risen Jesus

- Though greatly varied, what are the benefits of rites of passage? Why might cultures create such unique ways to initiate someone?
- Can you think of any ways that we can make sacramentality an active part of our church life?
- Pick one thing for the coming week that you can focus on being a visible sign of an invisible reality, and if you like, journal on how you see its connection to God.

Week VII
Vocation

Monday – Introducing Vocation

What were you created to do? What gives you energy? What makes you proud of what you can accomplish?

These questions are ways of opening up a sense of vocation. Certainly, your vocation can be your career. Our daughter, Griffin, has found her vocation in caring for animals, which she sees as a calling. She graduated from Vet School and serves as a Doctor of Veterinary Medicine. The great reformer Martin Luther revived a larger sense of vocation from a medieval view that saw vocation as referring explicitly to Holy Orders. Luther wrote, "Every occupation has its own honor before God. Ordinary work is a divine vocation or calling. In our daily work no matter how important or mundane we serve God by serving the neighbor and we also participate in God's on-going providence for the human race."

We know baristas, attorneys, artists, truck drivers,

Encountering the risen Jesus

The Way They Live is Thomas Anshutz' 1879 painting of a woman and her two children tending their own tobacco in West Virginia during Reconstruction.

teachers, real estate agents, and firefighters who live into their work as a vocation in that their work is an important place where their care and concern for others is made real. Seeing any work as a means of serving God is not about doing different things so much as doing all you do differently because you see the people you encounter as the neighbor who Jesus called you to love. The Rule of St. Benedict that set the early pattern for monks and nuns said, "All guests who present themselves are to be welcomed as Christ," in describing how to treat the stranger at the gate of the monastery. This describes the way we are to see the people we come across in our day. We know a retired chaplain who bagged groceries at the store to the glory of God, by praying for everyone checking out at the register and treating everyone with kind consideration.

This is vocation, but there is more to vocation than work. We know people who live into their vocation in their job that earns them a living, who also live into service to others in another way, such as serving in Kairos Prison Ministry or being an AA sponsor. A gifted nurse practitioner founded the Boy Scout troop at King of Peace, the church we started in Kingsland. Both the care of patients and serving as a mentor are among his vocations.

Your vocation can and should be every office and situation in life, so that the Reformer Martin Luther could talk of the vocation of marriage and also the vocation of celibacy. Either can be to the glory of God. For your vocation or vocations are the ways in which you use your God-given gifts in the service of God and the coming reign of God.

Our outer actions provide a means to walk the walk of our inner faith. Care shown for others is done with no thought to our gain, but in thanksgiving for all we have already been given. Having been saved by faith alone, without any need for works, we are free from the burden of earning God's love. Yet as followers of Jesus we have bound ourselves (freely) to living in service to others, not as a means of deserving that love, but in response to that love of God we see in Jesus. The Reformation sought to break down the sharp divide between the sacred and secular that had developed in Christian thought. Instead of those two separate realms, they saw the ordinary world in which we live being the place where we joyfully serve God in loving care for all creation.

In the Anglican tradition, we see how Archbishop Thomas Cranmer, who crafted the first Books of Common Prayer in English, in writing two Books of Homilies captured the same scriptural sense of faith and works in his sermons on Good Works and Idleness. He said that no one can buy or purchase heaven with his works, but that we should not be slack in doing good works, "seeing that it is the will of God that we should walk in them."

In the 'Prayers for Families to Use,' found in the first American Book of Common Prayer in 1789, there is an intercession: "Be gracious unto thy Church; and grant that every member of the same, in his vocation and ministry, may serve thee faithfully." This was to make it plain that every Christian shares a common call to serve God by serving others.

We also have different ages and stages of life and so we find new ways to live into vocation and ministry. The teacher or professor who is now a grandparent or great-grandparent finds new ways to use the same gifts and vocation in new ways. Each of us is blessed in giving to others from the gifts we have been given and retirement is a time for discovering that anew. New times in life give fresh opportunities for learning by doing and a great chance to take skills honed in previous seasons to use in an untried opportunity.

- If you are exploring a sense of what is your vocation at this stage in your life, ask: Where is my passion? What makes my heart sing? What gives me joy? How can I use this to serve God?
- How might you do what you already do differently out of this understanding of this being how you are to serve God in your daily life and work?

Tuesday – Victoria's Reflection

*"All people have access to their True Self
from their very first inhalation and exhalation,
which we now know is the very sound
of the sacred name Yahweh.
We breathe God in and out—
much more than we 'know' God,
understand God, or even talk to God."*

-Richard Rohr

Because my high school dream of being a hermit did not work out nor did I become a nun, I have pursued those vocations by pouring myself into my life as a Franciscan, and more importantly, into the meditation and quiet times of prayer that are a part of my Rule of Life. Keeping my mind quiet has always been a challenge because I have what is known as 'monkey brain'. My mind is constantly dashing from one thought to another. Yes, I have a little ADHD, and have to tell myself to focus at times, and it takes constant work, but I can accomplish that task.

Something that has really helped me, I first learned about in 2022—the breathing in and out of God's name. The concept made so much sense to me. I had already felt certain that God is the very air I breathe but to have it confirmed, to make my inhalations and exhalations have so much meaning, particularly when I am meditating, was life changing.

Numerous scholars and rabbis have noted that the letters YHWH represent the sounds of breathing, or if you prefer to think of it this way, aspirated consonants. When YHWH is pronounced without the intervening vowels, which, by the way, are just a guess, it actually sounds like breathing.

YH (inhale): WH (exhale).

It might help to know that in Hebrew, Y is pronounced yode and H is pronounced hey. I can hear it more clearly when I inhale when I think of it that way. Similarly, W is pronounced vav and the H is the same 'hey'.

Then, when you really consider it, you realize that when you are born, your first cry, your very first breath, is speaking the name of God.

When you sigh deeply, you call God's name. A whimper, a groan or even a gasp, a sob or a scream—any sound that is beyond words is still expressing the name of God.

Everything that breathes whether it be your enemy, an atheist, or even your favorite pet, declares God's name, when they inhale and exhale, even though they might be unaware

Holy Mysteries

that their very breath is giving constant acknowledgment to God.

And as you are born breathing the name of God, you will also leave this earth with your last breath, whispering God's name as your breath no longer fills your lungs.

This is such a beautiful thought that it's difficult not to get emotional when I sit and consider it. Our God chose to give itself a name that we cannot help but communicate every moment that we are alive.

Every living thing. Always and everywhere. Whether we are waking or sleeping, the name of God is an integral part of our lives.

Meditating on the name of God has made my time in silence so much more meaningful. It has also made it easier to see God in every living thing. Listening to the gentle snores of my cat, the squirrels chattering, or the birds singing and knowing they are one with their Creator makes me feel uniquely connected to them. And that's important because feeling connected to everyone, and everything, is what God wishes for us. It is only when we feel that connection that we can learn to love without boundaries, loving every creature, human or animal, as God does.

As Fyodor Dostoyevsky wrote in *The Brothers Karamazov*:

> "Love all God's creation, the whole and every grain of sand in it. Love every leaf, every ray of God's light. Love the animals, love the plants, love everything. If you love everything, you will perceive the divine mystery in things. Once you perceive it, you will

Encountering the risen Jesus

begin to understand it better every day. And you will come at last to love the whole world with an all-embracing love. … Things flow and are indirectly linked together, and if you push here, something will move at the other end of the world. If you strike here, something somewhere will wince; if you sin here, something somewhere will suffer."

- Have you felt a connection to all creation? When and how did that occur?
- What form of prayer nurtures you?

Wednesday – The Ascension

"So when they had come together, they asked him, 'Lord, is this the time when you will restore the kingdom to Israel?' He replied, 'It is not for you to know the times or periods that the Father has set by his own authority. But you will receive power when the Holy Spirit has come upon you; and you will be my witnesses in Jerusalem, in all Judea and Samaria, and to the ends of the earth.' When he had said this, as they were watching, he was lifted up, and a cloud took him out of their sight. While he was going and they were gazing up towards heaven, suddenly two men in white robes stood by them. They said, 'Men of Galilee, why do you stand looking up towards heaven? This Jesus, who has been taken up from you into heaven, will come in the same way as you saw him go into heaven.'" (Acts 1:6-11)

Holy Mysteries

This Ascension Day reading with the apostles looking up at Jesus' feet disappearing into the clouds can be a stumbling block. Some will remark rightly that we know better than to conceive of a three-storied universe with heaven above, hell beneath, and earth sandwiched in the middle. We have pierced the sky, traveled to the moon and are even now being watched over by astronauts working at the international space station. What sense does it make to talk of Jesus disappearing off into the sky, a vanishing point of distance from earth ending his earthly ministry?

This knowledge need not distract us as we know through our own faith journeys that God has a knack for giving us not just what we need, but what we are ready to receive. The disciples, or followers, were becoming apostles, or ones sent out, and they needed Jesus to leave in such a way that they would stop hanging around and get about the work of the Gospel. Ascension Day accomplished that essential purpose.

On all the days leading up to that one, the disciples looked for their Lord. Their lives were centered on Jesus. Knowing more about the heavens doesn't change the truth of Jesus' leaving his earthly ministry to become once more the second person of the Trinity, no longer limited by the incarnation to being in one place at a time. After the ascension, the apostles began to pray and wait for the coming of the Holy Spirit. Then with Pentecost, they were empowered to go out in ministry.

Ascension Day worked. With Jesus' ascension into heaven, the disciples were prepared to become apostles. They stopped looking for Jesus here and there, and began to pray for the Holy Spirit who would be with them always. On that day, Jesus' followers were given what they needed to begin to change their focus.

What would it take for us to change our focus? After all, it is easy for a church to go from being about the mission of sharing the love of God found in Jesus with a lost and hurting world to turning our mission stations into clubs. A church does not exist for its own sake, but as preparation for those who gather to take part in Christ's work of reconciliation in the world. The word "member" should probably not even be used for aligning oneself with a given congregation. We are not to be members of a club, exclusive or otherwise, as if Jesus' ministry, death and resurrection were for the purpose of starting a new institution. We are missionaries working on the front lines of the mission of the church, which is what we each encounter everywhere we go. The institution of the church exists to further the mission which is God's mission—reconciling the world to God.

This need to turn outward is so crucial. A commonly used dismissal for the Eucharist, "Go in peace to love and serve the Lord" is meant to be the equivalent to the two men robed in white who said, "Why do you stand looking up toward heaven?" The words of the angels turned the disciples' gaze outward to a lost and hurting world and so made them into apostles, ones sent forth on a mission. We too are to turn from being nourished spiritually at the altar to seeing the needs in the world around us anew because of our worship.

- In what ways is your congregation a social club?
- In what ways is your congregation furthering the mission of reconciling the world to God in Christ?

THURSDAY - QUOTATION

"In the winter, seeing a tree stripped of its leaves, and considering that within a little time the leaves would be renewed and after that the flowers and fruit appear, he received a high view of the Providence and Power of God, which has never since been effaced from his soul. That this view had perfectly set him loose from the world, and kindled in him such a love for God, that he could not tell whether it had increased during the more than forty years he had lived since."

This quotation is from the book, *Practicing the Presence of God*, written by the Cardinal de Noailles, Abbe Joseph de Beaufort, to collect his conversations with Brother Lawrence together with the monk's "maxims" and letters. In the first conversation, Lawrence recounted his conversion at age eighteen. Seeing the bare limbs of a tree standing out against a world shrouded in snow, he knew the tree would once again sprout leaves, then flowers and fruit. The certainty of the promise of this little resurrection of spring changed the course of his life; having discovered God's faithfulness, he joined the Discalced Carmelite monastery in Paris.

As a lay brother in the order, he served for 30 years as the cook in the monastery kitchen. Lawrence came to realize that God was present in the kitchen all the time. Yes, he could go to chapel and God would be present, but God was not just in the chapel. Right there in his kitchen, Lawrence became deeply aware of God's presence. The Cardinal described it this way in the book he compiled:

> "As Brother Lawrence had found such an advantage in walking in the presence of God, it was natural for him to recommend it earnestly to others; but his example was a stronger inducement than any arguments he could propose. His very countenance was edifying, such a sweet and calm devotion appearing in it as could not but affect the beholders. And it was observed that in the greatest hurry of business in the kitchen, he still preserved his recollection and heavenly-mindedness. He was never hasty nor loitering, but did each thing in its season, with an even, uninterrupted composure and tranquility of spirit. 'The time of business,' said he, 'does not with me differ from the time of prayer; and in the noise and clatter of my kitchen, while several persons are at the same time calling for different things, I possess God in as great tranquility as if I were upon my knees at the blessed sacrament.'"

The work of the kitchen was transformed by the unlearned monk when he realized that he did all of his work in the presence of God.

Holy Mysteries

- How might your daily life be different if you were always powerfully aware of God's presence?

Friday – Frank's Reflection

First, I wanted to be an astronaut. That earliest dream of "What I want to be when I grow up" lasted until at least fifth grade. But if I look to a hope that stuck with me, I don't recall a time before I aspired to be an Eagle Scout. I had started out in Cub Scouts before I was even old enough by attending my brothers' meetings as my Mom was the den mother. When I was finally old enough to be a Cub Scout, I joined and remained in scouting all through elementary school, junior high, high school, and my first year of college. Not only did I become an Eagle Scout, but I got my first tastes of travel in Scouting, twice backpacking out west at Philmont Scout Ranch, traveling to Sweden for the World Jamboree, working on the staff of the National Jamboree, and more.

I have often shared how my Scoutmaster, Gene McCord, was a larger than life figure in my youth. A lineman for the power company, he is a lifelong Southern Baptist, who connected his leadership in Scouting to his faith in God. Mr. McCord and the many other leaders who gave their time to our Scout Troop were my models for how I wanted to be as a Christian. I knew I would want to give back to God by paying forward the time and care they showed me, and I talked to Victoria about this when we met.

Encountering the risen Jesus

Frank reads a story to the kids in Children's Church at St. Peter's in Rome, Georgia, in early 1997.

In time, Victoria and I would work with the high school youth group at St. Peter's Episcopal Church in Rome, Georgia. This was our way of "paying forward" what the mentors in our lives had invested in us. We also began to serve in the children's chapel as our daughter, Griffin, was taking part in those child-friendly liturgies that took place during the Eucharist.

I remember so clearly arriving for a Sunday afternoon Bible Study full of doubts and fears as I wondered what to do with the strong call I felt to ordained ministry. I was worried about whether I was being a responsible husband and father

Holy Mysteries

to leave our current work of writing books and magazine articles freelance, to take on the heavy costs of three years of seminary. I got to the church early, and only one other person was there. Lea Taylor and I sat in a porch swing and talked. She said I seemed anxious and I told her that I was struggling with a decision and I needed prayer. She said, "You need to read the Sermon on the Mount." Frankly, it sounded like pat advice that did not apply to my concerns. I replied, "You mean in Matthew?" thinking of the beatitudes with the familiar, "Blessed are the meek for they shall inherit the earth," and all the rest. Lea said, "No, in Luke." I told her that I would read it and then she startled me by handing me her Bible. She would not wait. Lea is a dear sweet soul and is not usually so forceful. It got my attention. I took the Bible and read in Luke chapter 12 starting at verse 27 where she pointed me. It reads, "Consider the lilies, how they grow: they neither toil nor spin; yet I tell you even Solomon in all his glory was not clothed like one of these. But if God so clothes the grass of the field, which is alive today and tomorrow is thrown into the oven, how much more will he clothe you—you of little faith!"

I kept reading scarcely believing my eyes, "And do not keep striving for what you are to eat and what you are to drink, and do not keep worrying. For it is the nations of the world that strive after all these things, and your Father knows you need them. Instead strive for his kingdom, and these things will be given to you as well." I may be thickheaded, but I know enough to feel a 2x4 when it hits me between the eyes. God had taken away my final excuse.

God was faithful to that promise and we were able to go to seminary, even traveling to Africa and Israel during those three years, without building up school loans to bring back to Georgia. This allowed us to go to work for the diocesan minimum salary in accepting the call to start a new church in Kingsland.

The call had not been to something higher or better, but a call to live into being who God made me to be. Through responding to the mentorship roles God had long called me to, I was able to discover what else the Holy Spirit had in mind for me. I have experienced many times in which the Spirit has used others to tell me what I needed to hear, just as Lea handed me Luke's Gospel that day.

- What did you first want to be when you grew up?
- How have you experienced the Spirit using others to speak to you?

SATURDAY – PENTECOST

"When the day of Pentecost had come, the disciples were all together in one place. And suddenly from heaven there came a sound like the rush of a violent wind, and it filled the entire house where they were sitting. Divided tongues, as of fire, appeared among them, and a tongue rested on each of them. All of them were filled with the Holy Spirit and began to speak in other languages, as the Spirit gave them ability. Now there were devout Jews from every nation under heaven living in Jerusalem. And at this sound the crowd gathered and was bewildered, because each one heard them speaking in the native language of each. Amazed and astonished, they asked, "Are not all these who are speaking Galileans? And how is it that we hear, each of us, in our own native language? Parthians, Medes, Elamites, and residents of Mesopotamia, Judea and Cappadocia, Pontus and Asia, Phrygia and Pamphylia, Egypt and the parts of Libya belonging to Cyrene, and visitors from Rome, both Jews and proselytes, Cretans and Arabs—in our own languages we hear them speaking about God's deeds of power." All were amazed and perplexed, saying to one another, "What does this mean?" (Acts 2:1-12)

This is an ongoing tendency in the post-Enlightenment West to treat phenomena for which we have no ready understanding with a heavy dose of reductionism. The physicist turned Anglican priest, John Polkinghorne, said in his book *Quarks, Chaos and Christianity*, some people are "nothing butters" when it comes to the world we live in. Reductionists see a thing as "nothing but" its physical explanation. They need only look at the most elemental form of a thing to explain everything.

For someone with a "nothing butter" way of making sense of the world, the compositions of Bach and Beethoven are nothing but vibrations that interact with our eardrums to create the effect we call music. The Mona Lisa is nothing but flecks of paint that we experience as differing colors. Baptism is nothing but water poured over someone's head as a part of a ritual observance. The Eucharist is nothing but bread and wine and the Pentecost experience was nothing but religious hysteria.

Yes, Bach and Beethoven's greatest works do reach our ears as nothing but vibrations against our eardrums, for that is how the beauty of the composers' work is transmitted. But you can't reduce their music to mere vibrations hitting your eardrum. Nor can the Mona Lisa's enigmatic smile be understood solely by describing the paint and the canvas. In these works of art, the notes of music and the paint on the canvas convey so much more, that reducing them to the essential physical phenomena misses the point.

So also, the Pentecost experience of the Holy Spirit coming to Jesus' disciples on that fiftieth day after the Passover, would have created some emotionalism akin to religious hysteria. Yet whatever caused some in the crowd that day to wonder whether the disciples had been drinking, was not all there was to the event. We know that there was something more because of the immediate and the lasting impact of that day. The immediate effect was to begin sharing the Good News of Jesus with those who were far off as well as with those who were near to the Jewish faith.

The Pentecost event defied any "it was nothing but" explanation. We can't reduce Pentecost to "It was nothing but emotionalism," or "It was nothing but mass hysteria," or even "It was nothing but a long-ago event we can no longer explain." The closest we can get is "Pentecost was nothing less

Holy Mysteries

than the presence of God." That day, the Jesus Movement was transformed not by human will, but by an act of the Holy Spirit. For while the apostles first gathered out of fear, this same ragtag band of disciples will bust out of this room, take to the streets, and tell the world about Jesus. Within a few generations the Good News of their resurrected Lord will be known throughout the Roman Empire and in time it will go out to the ends of the earth, all through the work of the Holy Spirit.

Pentecost is a time to remember that God's spirit is still present in a mighty way. That's why our worship can't be reduced to "nothing but" music, readings and a sermon. The Eucharist can never be described as "nothing but" bread and wine, any more than baptism is "nothing but" water and words. That is far too limiting. We don't want "nothing but" a religious experience. We long for nothing less than the power and presence of God, a presence for which you were created and for which your soul longs.

We see in this explosive event how God used what was already present. It was new that the first followers of Jesus preached fluently on that Pentecost "as the Spirit gave them ability." But it is aso significant that there were gifts we had already seen present in the gaggle of Galileans. Simon, who Jesus called Peter, already had the can-do spirit to step out of a boat onto the water. He was often wrong, but always ready to act. Thomas had the backbone to name his doubts. Philip was already bringing those beyond Judaism in to see Jesus. They had abilities and passions that God knew could and would be used in the earliest days of what would become

Encountering the risen Jesus

Christianity. But what they required was the inspiration, the prompting of the Holy Spirit, that gave them new abilities for language that they needed, and added to their existing gifts that morning.

- How might the Holy Spirit be prompting you to use your gifts in new ways?

Pentecost – Vocation Revisited

In our Gospel reading for our worship today, Jesus tells his disciples, "If you love me, you will keep my commandments." Jesus said these words on the night before he died, calling his followers to love him through doing what he has commanded. This is the same night in which Jesus said, "I give you a new commandment, that you love one another. Just as I have loved you, you also should love one another. By this everyone will know that you are my disciples, if you have love for one another.'"

Reading John, chapters 13-14, provides the context in which Jesus is preparing the disciples for their lives that will follow his death, resurrection, and ascension. He emphasizes the most important lesson, the one his whole life and ministry made clear, we are to love God and love our neighbors as ourselves. Everything else in all scripture is a commentary on this call to love.

Earlier in this passage, Jesus said, "As the Father has loved me, so I have loved you; abide in my love. If you keep my commandments, you will abide in my love, just as I have kept my Father's commandments and abide in his love." The goal here is to abide in love. Abide means to stay, to remain, to dwell, or even to hang out. Jesus is not teaching that if we don't do everything he commands, he won't love us anymore. Rather, if we long to abide in the love of God, we should follow the example of Jesus' words and actions. To remain in, dwell in, live in the love of God is to live the life Jesus taught us to live. This is the life that bears fruit that will last.

This is also the one vocation all Christians share—love. We are to love God and love our neighbors as ourselves. This vocation of love is one that works best with learning by doing rather than reading and meditating alone. Want to learn how to love, then practice love. Of course, this doesn't mean that you must feel a particular emotion toward someone. Love is a decision, an act of will. Love is best learned by putting love into action. In fact, loving those who are difficult to love can only be learned in practice. The love Jesus both taught and lived cost him his life, so this is love beyond mere sentimentality or emotion. Jesus teaches about the form of love that in Greek is called *agape*. This is a self-giving love, which is more concerned about the other person than oneself. *Agape* love starts with God, and God's love for us. With this love of God and God's love for me, I can then begin to see other people as God sees them. I can even begin to see myself as God sees me. From this experience, I reach out in love to others with the love that begins in the very life and nature of God.

Encountering the risen Jesus

Our Gospel reading for today also tells us that Jesus promises to send an Advocate, the Holy Spirit saying, "You know him, because he abides with you, and he will be in you." In our call to love others as Jesus loves, we have the Holy Spirit to guide us and support us.

Your life in Christ brings joy when you find the ways to combine the gifts God has given you with the love we are all to have and share. When you let the Holy Spirit guide you, opportunities to show love of God will come up and they won't be the ways someone else is called to love. For one person, it could be cutting a neighbor's grass while they go through chemotherapy or assisting a neighbor with a car repair so they can continue to have transportation to work. For someone else it will be sitting with someone in grief. For yet another person, it will be in starting a new ministry that impacts hundreds or thousands of people. None of this is one-size fits all, as each of us is a unique individual. The common call is to a great variety of ways of sharing the love of God we have found in Jesus.

We were made to love. When we share the love of God with others, the world is transformed. In the process, our hearts are transformed more fully by the love of God flowing through us toward others. And in this common vocation to love, we find joy.

- How have you used your unique gifts to show love to someone else?
- Pray for an opportunity to put love into action in the coming weeks.

EPILOGUE – THE ROAD TO DAMASCUS

"Meanwhile Saul, still breathing threats and murder against the disciples of the Lord, went to the high priest and asked him for letters to the synagogues at Damascus, so that if he found any who belonged to the Way, men or women, he might bring them bound to Jerusalem. Now as he was going along and approaching Damascus, suddenly a light from heaven flashed around him. He fell to the ground and heard a voice saying to him, 'Saul, Saul, why do you persecute me?' He asked, 'Who are you, Lord?' The reply came, 'I am Jesus, whom you are persecuting. But get up and enter the city, and you will be told what you are to do.' The men who were traveling with him stood speechless because they heard the voice but saw no one. Saul got up from the ground, and though his eyes were open, he could see nothing; so they led him by the hand and brought him into Damascus. For three days he was without sight, and neither ate nor drank." (Acts 9:1-9)

Saul lies in the dust on the road to Damascus. Stopped in his angry tracks by a light from heaven that flashes around him, he hears a voice saying, "Saul, Saul, why do you persecute me?"

Saul now knows that everything he once knew with certainty was an illusion. He thought he was fighting the heretics on behalf of a vengeful God. His self-righteous quest was designed to both appease an angry God and propel him

Encountering the risen Jesus

The Conversion of Saint Paul by Benozzo Gozzoli (c. 1460s)

into the religious elite. His rigid religiosity left him blinded to the grace of God found in Jesus.

Then God speaks to Ananias in a vision to send him to Saul. When Ananias lays hands on him, Saul has something like scales fall from his eyes. Saul awakens from the nightmare, to see the world anew.

In a carefully crafted passage in his Letter to the Philippians, the one-time persecutor of those on The Way writes, "Let the same mind be in you that was in Christ Jesus."

Paul is writing about *metanoia*, which literally means to have an "after mind" or your mind after being reconfigured in a metamorphosis like the one he experienced on the road to Damascus. We describe this type of transformation as a change of heart and mind. Translators like to opt for the most economical way of conveying a concept with a single word standing in for another single word. So that the word repent stood in for a change in how someone sees the world and their place in it. Jesus began his public ministry with the brief proclamation: "The time is fulfilled, and the kingdom of God has come near; repent, and believe in the good news."

When we read the word "repent" in scripture, it helps to recall this is *metanoia* in the original Greek and while it encompasses repentance, the word is more full of meaning than the English translation reveals. The aftermind or converted or transformed mind refers to seeing everything in a completely new way. This is more like waking from a nightmare to see the world rightly. This change of heart was perhaps best captured in a Neil Diamond song made into a hit by The Monkees. It became a hit again thanks to the greatest movie credits of all time at the end of Shrek.

> I thought love was only true in fairy tales
> Meant for someone else, but not for me
> Love was out to get me
> That's the way it seemed
> Disappointment haunted all my dreams

This is a description of the Before Mind. Our thinking pattern

Encountering the risen Jesus

before the metamorphosis. Then a moment in time causes the singer to have their perceptions of the world changed forever. This After Mind is described in this unforgettable chorus:

> Then I saw her face, now I'm a believer
> Not a trace of doubt in my mind
> I'm in love
> I'm a believer, I couldn't leave her if I tried

This same transformation happens to Saul when he encounters Jesus, comes to know him for who he is, and falls in love. This change of heart and mind is what happens to Andrew, Simon Peter, James, and John that has them walk away from their nets. This moment of recognition of the truth of the Good News of Jesus changes the heart of Mary Magdalene, who becomes the apostle to the apostles after Jesus' resurrection. This change in seeing the world causes the first followers of Jesus to face persecution and even death for the love of God they had found in their savior. Down through the centuries, we see saints in every age in whose lives we find a *metanoia*, a revolution, that takes over their hearts and minds after which life is never, ever the same.

The first followers of Jesus came to know that love is not only true in fairy tales when the risen Jesus appeared to them demonstrating that nothing, not even death, can stop God's love. The message of Eastertide is that while everything that needs to be done has already been done by Jesus, we can respond more fully to what the Holy Trinity has done

Holy Mysteries

through our Savior. The metamorphosis is not simply a one-time experience, but ongoing Holy Spirit work. You can't earn it. You can't deserve it, but you can continually receive more. We see this expectation of more to come in the early Christian Church tradition of teaching mystagogy not about a one-time revelation of something that had been hidden, but as an important turning point in an ever-deepening understanding of something we know in part. This *metanoia* is meant to be ongoing as we conform our lives closer to Christ. And while one can certainly become more like Jesus on one's own, the life of faith is best lived in community.

We hope that reflecting on the sacraments, the resurrection appearances in scripture, quotations from important witnesses to this season of the Church Year, and our reflections on how we have encountered Jesus has indeed prompted you to look for the ways, both mundane and surprising, that you have experienced the risen Jesus. Our hope has been that you will be encouraged to see how the Holy Spirit has been with you in the past which gives you added trust that God will continue to be with you in the future, from this life to the life eternal.

www.ingramcontent.com/pod-product-compliance
Lightning Source LLC
Chambersburg PA
CBHW070427010526
44118CB00014B/1932